A Mother's Journey
of
Love, Death, and Forgiveness

Losing Our Thirty-Three-Year-Old Son in a Car Accident...

Faith, Hope, and Unconditional Love

Jackie Loret de Mola

DORRANCE
PUBLISHING CO
EST. 1920
PITTSBURGH, PENNSYLVANIA 15238

Dorrance Publishing Co
585 Alpha Drive
Pittsburgh, PA 15238
Visit our website at dorrancebookstore.com

ISBN: 978-1-6470-2231-0
eISBN: 978-1-6470-2888-6

Preface

When I began thinking about writing this book, I just wasn't sure I could do it. I kept hearing a real nudging in my head and heart that I like to call the Holy Spirit. I thought about how I would share my real pain and suffering over the death of my son, Frank, and also the true joy that came because of his loss.

While I was visiting my mom in Tucson, Arizona, I met my friend Annie Mammen at Cracker Barrel. Annie asked me to share all the Facebook posts I wrote since the day of Frank's car accident and assemble a book. She told me about a man she met while flying to see her dad in El Paso who had written a book about his young son's death, also in a car accident. I told her I had been thinking of doing just that. I felt like I didn't need any more confirmation than that! But it would take months for me to get the strength and motivation to actually even re-read what I wrote, which is so painful and real.

And so, it is...over a year later and I am finally putting my words together in hope of helping others—especially moms who have lost their child or children. I hope it helps others too.

Also, I have a friend who has inspired me to share my words, as she has done the same. Pat Berg, author of *Handle it with Prayer*, has lived this process and knows how to write her gut feelings on paper so others can see Faith in Action!

My faith has been my rock throughout my life and through this process of death, forgiveness, donor recipients, and rebirth. I hope you can find even one sentence of this book that can help you cry through the pain to look forward to the day when tears are wiped away, or at least made easier.

I want to thank so many people who have been by my side through this incredible journey: my husband of forty-four-plus years, Enrique, who held me many nights as I wept myself to sleep and patiently waited for better days. Our sons, Nicolas, Alex, and David, who miss their brother in a way I don't even understand. I still have my five siblings. My beautiful mother, Laura, who has been willing to fly out when I thought I couldn't make it through another day. My friend, Carlota Agard, who held me when I cried, even in airport bathrooms. My friend Sandi Austin, who is my Tucson rock and my positivity when I felt I couldn't move forward. My numerous friends across the country who have given me e-hugs in the hundreds. My friend Nancy Tran, who kept me doing things to get me out of the house on Mondays and Wednesdays. My siblings, Phil, Anna, Betty, Tricia, Gary, Paul, Irma, Kathleen, and Steve, who shared my pain but got me to laugh. My uncles, aunts, cousins, nieces, and nephews who are the makeup of love, and my grandchildren who spent many lazy weekends and days loving me through all of this, patiently waiting for Nana to get up from the recliner to do something with them. I owe you trips to the zoo and so much more! I love all of you!

Thank you to Gus and Michelle Lloyd, who walked me through Jerusalem just weeks after Frank's death. I quote Gus often in this book, and you can see him online at GusLloyd.com or listen to him early in the morning on Sirius XM Catholic Channel 129. Thank you so much for allowing me to quote you! You have strengthened my spiritual life!

And now to the God who made me...Thank You, Father! Thank You for allowing me to scream at You more than once! Thank You for allowing the Blessed Mother to hold me and take Franko under her arms, like I begged of her. I feel Frank's presence is here and in heaven. Thank You, Jesus, for being in me! When I receive You in Holy Communion, I KNOW You are dwelling in me. Your very presence illuminates my life from the inside out because of grace. Thank You Holy Spirit for giving me the gumption to write and create with the gifts You bestowed on me very long ago! I write, sing, and play my guitar because of You! Thank you!

For A Bereaved Mother

Mary, what can I say now that my child is gone?
Mother of Sorrows, to you I turn for help and comfort.
I have lost my child, just as you lost your son Jesus
when you stood beneath the cross and saw him die for our sins.
You suffered so much, Mary, and you must know what I am suffering.
I do not understand why God has allowed this sorrow to
come into my life; yet I know that He is my loving father
and that He is all good. I must be patient and trustful.
Heavenly Mother, pray that I may have strength.

What are those words, so gentle and consoling, I seem to hear you say?
Yes, my child is happy in heaven. Some day we are going to meet again
where there will be no more sadness, no more parting.
Until then I will look to you holding your divine Son in your arms
and I know you will help me to understand and bear my sorrow.

And now begins a new chapter…life without Frank Anthony Loret de Mola. I love you, my son. I miss you, my son. I'll see you again, in God's time!

David, our youngest son, put this on Facebook. Frank wrote it:

Frank Loret de Mola —

"What feeds this—the search to fulfill the potential of our beings—which is as bore or boundless weaknesses, then take the scraps and smelt them to ore to make better boots, and call in your friends to mix more concrete to pour yourself into.

Our relationships with others make the mortar, but the brick—that's the stacking of experience.

But what is the sunlight that guides us as its light blinds us to the intent of our everyday actions?"

On the morning of 9/20/2017, I posted this meditation on Facebook early in the morning...before we knew...

MEDITATION OF THE DAY

"There is another reason also why the soul has traveled safely in this obscurity; it has suffered: for the way of suffering is safer, and also more profitable, than that of rejoicing and of action. In suffering God gives strength, but in action and in joy the soul does but show its own weakness and imperfections. And in suffering, the soul practices and acquires virtue, and becomes pure, wiser, and more cautious."

— St. John of the Cross

Remembering 9/20/17 as I write on 3/27/19:

We didn't find out about our son's accident until 5:00 P.M. on 9/20/17. By the time we got to San Joaquin General Hospital, he had been there for about five hours.

Frank had recently moved in with his girlfriend/partner at a place she had rented. Her roommate moved out, and Frank agreed to move in, after much contemplation. He was a procrastinator, so it didn't surprise us that the California Highway Patrol needed help from the Sacramento Police Department to find Frank. His license showed his old address, and it also showed he was an organ donor.

Frank lived in an apartment across the street from the roasting plant/Naked Coffee prior to moving to his girlfriend's apartment. He worked for Naked Coffee. (Naked coffee is coffee roasted without chemicals. Just wanted to be clear as to the "naked" part of the coffee company.) Frank was driving to or from a business meeting when he was in the accident.

Frank's last known address was near his work, and when the Sacramento PD officer knocked on the door of the apartment, the new renter was able to tell the Sac PD that Frank worked across the street. The officer went to the roasting plant and asked if anyone had Frank Loret de Mola's parents' phone number. The owner of the company, Chris, said no, but he knew someone who might have the number. Chris called AJ, a manager at the Naked Lounge, and she said she didn't have any phone numbers. AJ said, "Frank's brother David just happens to be here, and he could talk." David got the news first.

David had to get to the hospital fast, but he first picked up Frank's girlfriend, and drove to San Joaquin General Hospital about one and three-fourth hours away. Frank was in Manteca, California when the accident happened. That is why he was taken to San Joaquin. His girlfriend called to tell me she and David were on their way to the hospital, and she was very scared. Since our granddaughter was at our house, I called her mom, Jennifer, to come and pick her up as soon as she could. We told her we had to hurry to get to the hospital and we didn't know what condition Frank was in. She got to our house very quickly, and we left to see our son.

Henry and I got on the road, and we were very quiet. Then we both said we felt this was not good. We said a rosary. We cried. I wanted to scream. We both knew, we both felt...he was already in heaven. Franko would have called us to say, "No worries, it's all good." He said that to us often.

Getting to the hospital took forever, it seemed. Once we got there, we were not able to see Frank for about forty-five minutes. It made zero sense. Frank's boss, Chris, and his girlfriend were waiting. They hadn't seen him either. David was the only one allowed to be in the room with Frank. We understood they only allowed next of kin.

Nobody was telling us anything as we waited. Then suddenly David came out...eyes beet red. Tears obviously everywhere on him. Then as quickly as he was there, he ran back in. About ten minutes later he came out with the doctor. The doctor, an emergency room neurosurgeon, asked us to follow him. Later David told us that he told the doctor to speak to us in a better way than how he spoke to him when giving him the news. Sometimes ER doctors are very matter of fact, forgetting they have human beings on the other side of disaster!

I have worked in the medical world most of my working career, so I know a bit too much. I realized that the doctor was not going to let us see our son...He walked us to a grieving room, and I began to yell, "No! No!

No!" We went into a room with couches, and he began to tell us that he had a traumatic brain injury and that his brain was extremely swollen. I said, "Can't you drill holes and drain his brain?"

He said, "There is nothing we can do. This type of brain injury doesn't get better. His brain stem was severed."

"WHAT? WHAT DID YOU SAY?" The doctor left us there to gain some sort of composure…whatever that is! And soon we were walked to a room where Frank was. He looked beautiful! He looked peaceful. He looked gorgeous. Not a scratch. Not a mark. Not a cut or bruise. How can this be? Later we learned that the way his car was hit made the injury more severe than had he been hit straight on in the rear. He was hit on the rear driver's side, and he hit a car that was stopped in front of him. He was at a complete stop as well.

Soon Frank was moved to ICU, and that would be his final place for his stay. We were told that we could stay with him all day and all night. We were told that everyone could be in the room at the same time. Only one nurse had to be informed that we were allowed to all be in his room, and we never had another issue. They were all wonderful to us and to Franko.

It is hard to believe that we were only there for two days. In two days so much happened, and a lot of that is now a blur. I have a huge regret, that David had to be the one to i.d. his brother. Yes, Frank looked great…but he never responded to any stimulation or even when they tested him for brain death, and took him off of life support, he didn't flinch. Nothing…I wish David didn't have to handle any of this. But he did, and I wish it was me.

So much happened at the hospital—agreements and disagreements on how things should be done, hugs and kisses, and stress beyond belief. We were trying to be respectful of everyone's feelings but wanted the best in all ways for our son. There were questions about spirituality, what he believed or didn't, and if we would respect his wishes to be a donor and be cremated. NO parent should have to make these decisions, but we were the people who had to do it…legally…and we wouldn't have wanted it any other way. Henry asked for a priest for anointing of the sick. The priest came and blessed Frankie, and our hearts felt a sense of relief. It wasn't for Frank, really. It was for us.

Frank had a very close friend, Father Joshua Lickter. Frank helped Fr. Josh build his coffee shop called The Fig Tree in Roseville, California, and he sold the Naked Coffee brand to Fr. Josh, along with all training for staff. Frank even helped paint and put up wall hangings and more. Part of the coffee shop was used for Mass on Sundays and live music daily. Franko had a huge part in all of the building and supplying of The Fig Tree. Relationships were built with Fr. Josh, his wife Rachel, and their son, Elliott. They still miss our son so much!

Father Joshua came into Frank's room at God's perfect timing. He calmed all fears and brought peace. He and his wife Rachel brought Jesus to the room, and we prayed, he blessed Frankie, and we sang, "Prayer of St. Francis." "Make me a channel of Your peace. Where there is hatred, let me bring Your love." This song epitomizes our son. He lived this song. Father Josh said Frank was more Christian than most Christians. We learned more and more about that truth as the days went on.

Many of Franko's friends came to see him. We heard several men say, "Frank made me a better man!" Women kissed him and told him they loved him and thank you! As I think about those days, I am in awe of the life of our son and his thirty-three years and all the love created because of one beautiful soul. Hundreds came for his funeral. People from all walks of life and from all over the world: China, England, Washington, Canada, Arizona, and more. His life was lived fully. He is missed tremendously.

I know life continues, but I doubt I will ever get over Frank's death. Even writing this almost makes no sense. How can this be happening? But it has and now you can share in my journal of love, death, and forgiveness.

My Journey:
My Journal Begins

9/20/17

I took down the posts about Frank. Just know how much we appreciate all the prayers and love.

Maybe the answer to prayer isn't what we want...let go of what I want and open the infinite door that awaits us all!

Our family is going through something that is a nightmare. Our son, Frank, was in a car accident yesterday. He was unconscious when paramedics arrived. They knew from the position he was in, his eyes, that he was gone. He is still alive. Alex was able to fly out immediately. Nick is on his way home, and things are being done medically so he hangs in there for some family and friends to see him. I love everyone so much, but I can't possibly answer everyone. It is overwhelming to say the least. I will post with any changes. Henry and I are with him and not leaving him except for an hour here or two hours there. Please know that I will reach out soon. I love you. Thank you! God bless you and pray for Frank Loret de Mola! Please!

9/21/17

STAT CT scan now to compare yesterday to today…then a second opinion from the head of neurosurgery. Pray more for us, thank you!

Later at night on 9/21/17

Sleep. No bed bugs at least! Goodnight Enrique Loret de Mola, my sons, Nick Loret de Mola, Alex Loret de Mola, Frank Loret de Mola, David Loret de Mola. I love you so much! We can do this together. His girlfriend, and Jennifer Loret de Mola, and Allie Criado…we need each other. Peace be with you all. Frank would want that! I love you!

Nothing but love! God, I love you my Son!

From Frank's Grammy, my Mom, Laura Loebe:

My handsome Frankie. You bring such joy to me. I love you forever. Grammy.

9/22/17 morning

Oh God I want him back NOW!!!! GOD! CAN YOU HEAR ME? Believers and non-believers alike can unite in this...WE LOVE THIS HUMAN BEING! THIS INCREDIBLE MAN MY SON Frank Loret de Mola! Why is he going? I know we were not meant to live in this form on Earth forever...but I know and I believe that we continue to be a part of each other's lives after we aren't on this planet any longer. BUT...WHY AT 33 YEARS OF AGE DOES HE HAVE TO GO? Does someone know why? The answer isn't easy. The answer isn't something anyone can easily grasp. The answer is far too deep to WANT to believe it. But if I didn't believe in a life Eternal...what is left? I will be so bold to say...I know I will see Frank, our son, in my dreams. I know I will see Frank, our son, when I am at a grocery store or walking down the street, and someone is walking like him or looks like him or has his heart, kidneys, or his skin. And do you know what I will see? Love...joy...smiles from our son. My pain is so real. I cannot sleep. My heart is laid open. I cannot imagine life without you, Franko. My ears hear your laughter when you and your brothers are enjoying your time together...loudly! My soul begs God to not take you... take me instead!

SO...NO ANSWERS TO WHY? This beautiful man we call Son, Brother, Lover, Friend, has left a beautiful legacy of love, peace, harmony, truth, encouragement, and joy like we have never known...I call all of that God...known to me through the sons I gave birth to. I call Franko a Jesus living and walking, a belief and love of humanity. I call Franko a Holy Spirit person who blessed his family and friends with memories to continue his legacy of love in action.

I call him life.   Amen!

9/22/17 later morning

This is love...need I say more?

9/23/17

Frank Loret de Mola, our incredible son, has left us...broken hearted, sad beyond belief, and thanking God for His life of love. If you have never had an opportunity to meet our son, just look at his Facebook page...love never ends. Tears fall and stop and fall and stop. How will life look from here on...?

I will hold him in my heart. I will trust God's design on my life and take time to heal. A lot of time. Remember his laugh, remember his eyes. Remember his hair, but mostly please remember...remember...remember! I gave birth to him...I will never forget!

I am Frank's Mom Forever!

Later on 9/23/17

I have said this to a few friends...My heart is in pieces, but Jesus is putting me back together...very slowly.

I know we say, "Kiss your family and friends because you never know when you can't any more." It is now all too real...We lost our third son...but we gained a light that shines so bright. I bet his light will create a new universe for scientists to explore, and his light will enlighten all who find him. And I am talking about Frank Loret de Mola...but this is really about a God who loves us and holds us firmly in His hands to protect us and get us through the hardest times in our lives. HE is the light. HE is the truth. How do Enrique Loret de Mola and I get through this? One minute at a time. Even one second at a time...with the love of Jesus...I send to all of you my deepest love and sorrowful thoughts for your loss too.

My Son moved people who met him to make a better path, take a new look at life. Dance while you cry, sing when there's nothing else you can do, walk with a little kick in your step, hug as if you can't let go ever, listen when you feel there is no room in your heart for words, and then listen some more, dream your dreams, make a new way, and just love until it hurts. We are hurting so deep in our souls, but in that place, we have room for all! I love you, my Frank, and my whole being knows you are forever with me.

One of Frank Loret de Mola's college friends shared a BUNCH of pictures and videos of my Franko! This is HYSTERICAL! I wish I was a fly on the wall in his life!

Friends are important because...
"you share affection and attention, and those are the two things that every human being (especially me!) needs to have in order to live with themselves. Also, they are good people to drink with!"
-Frank Loret de Mola

God is good. God is love. During this tragic time, it's easy for me and my family to forget that, but we can't lose sight that God loves us. Wish we could play another round of poker. I love you Franko, forever. Rest easy. This is a picture of Frank that Sandi made my necklace out of.

9/25/17

We are so thankful for hundreds of people who know and will forever love our son, Frank Loret de Mola! We are in shock, and the pain of losing our beautiful baby is unfathomable...It feels like a very bad dream. But sadly, it isn't.

One thing I ask...The viewing/vigil will take place in a very holy place. I ask that all of us (me included because I don't want to get angry again with God in His House...as I have at home) to be respectful...No bad words spoken...Stories of Frank are welcomed, but keep the stories clean, please.

I am in awe of his blessed community of people we now call our family! Because there is an 8:00 A.M. morning Mass, no one can get to the church until 8:30.

The services for our son Frank had to be moved to Friday, September 29, at nine to eleven, viewing at St. Paul, and at eleven the mass will begin. The church is located at 8720 Florin Rd. Sacramento, CA 95829.

If you would like to send flowers, in honor of our son Frank Loret de Mola, please consider donating to the Brain Trauma Foundation at: Brain Trauma Foundation

Thank you!

Jackie Loebe Loret de Mola and Enrique Loret de Mola

Still 9/25/17

This was day three without Frank Loret de Mola...Still not understanding why but willing to trust some sort of plan.

I know life will get better, but I won't be the same anymore. I will be better. I will love even strangers more. I will have more compassion. I will live like it's my last day on Earth. I will love my husband more. I will love our sons more and learn from them how to live in that love. Of all the people in our world, it was not Frank's time...but it was...really was. Through his death, people have come together. Through his death, I have seen the reason why we didn't see him as much as we wanted, because he was so busy loving the world, playing and teaching and being a true servant of peace. I am so proud of the man I called my baby! How blessed I was to give birth to one so wonderful and special and full of joy.

I love you Frank Anthony Loret de Mola!

9/26/17

His love was limitless. His laugh permeated the walls. His heart, liver, and kidneys NOW are in people who will be well again! I love you, my baby. I miss you and I ache...and ache...and ache...

Rachel, Frank, and Ashley, Cousins

David shared this picture of him behind Franko, and Frank's acting like David's choking him.

A typical joking around moment! I love this, Son! Thank you! Made me happy if only for a while.

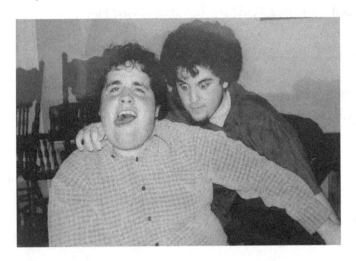

Jesse Lowther...my New Hampshire son...I love you so much! Frank loved you and your brother! I can't believe this gift you are giving by coming for Frank Loret de Mola!!!!! Thank you for your love.

More on 9/26/17

Goodnight my family and friends. God bless you. Peace be with you. Please stay safe. Shine your light so all the world can see! Shine it so bright that my eyes will see you in New Hampshire, Pennsylvania, Maine, Vermont, Michigan, Chicago, Texas, Montana, Hawaii, Philippines, China, Jerusalem, Arizona, California, and all the places in between. And when you shine your light, blow a kiss to the universe toward Frank Loret de Mola! I bet he will catch it!!!! Then do some kind of arms raised, laughing kind of dance to show he truly is number one!

Sleep with the angels, my love. And as I would pray with you when you were so little:

"Now I lay me down to sleep. I pray the Lord my soul to keep. Guard me Jesus through the night and wake me with the morning light. God bless daddy. God bless Mommy. God bless Nicolas. God bless Alex. God bless David. And God bless me!"

And then I would sing:

"You are so beautiful to me. You are so beautiful to me, can't you see? You're everything I hoped for. You're everything I need. You are so beautiful...to...me."

I sang that to each of our sons. I still have that in my head throughout the years. Can you sing it again, Mommy? Yes Baby...I am.

I love you, Frank Anthony, to the end of the earth!

And I posted for Nicolas, but he wasn't ready to even see birthday wishes.

Happy almost birthday to our oldest son, Nick Loret de Mola. In this time, we want to give honor to a son whom we love unconditionally, who has given us the loves of our lives in Jacob and Emma. God gave you to us because we need you, Son. God bless you in the early morning on Wednesday, September 27th! I love you!!!!!

9/27/17

Frank posted this on 9/27/16:

My girlfriend and I caught by my mom Jackie Loebe Loret de Mola at my brother David And Yes Loret de Mola's show. Bought an album. He drops serious fire, man.

9/28/17

And in the end…when all is stripped away and our hearts are opened to exposed souls, what is left? Love. Love. Love. Frank Loret de Mola is love, was love, professed love, breathed love, inhaled love, sang love, heard love, lived love, adopted love, rejoiced in love, believed in love, knew love, encountered love, loved love. His loss is attached to me now like a leaf on a tree…so simple but so complex. Franko, if I could have taken your place… I still would. But this stupid thing called death has done incredible things to your old mom. I feel your light. I feel your love. I feel your presence with all of us, and that remains…your spirit of love.

> "Let us make up for lost time. Let us give to God the time that remains to us."
>
> — St. Alphonsus Liguori

Most days, my morning ritual is reading my email and meditating on all things Trinity and the Blessed Mother.

Today's Verse of the Day is so powerful, and it is about the person our son Frank Loret de Mola is. Take time to meditate on this…reflect on this… and thank our Creator for Franko.

> VERSE OF THE DAY
> "I therefore, the prisoner in the Lord, beg you to lead a life worthy of the calling to which you have been called, with all humility and gentleness, with patience, bearing with one another in love, making every effort to maintain the unity of the Spirit in the bond of peace."
>
> — Ephesians 4:1-3

This song takes on new meaning for me now. I think of my dad, who died in 2008…but now…but now. My lover boy Frank Loret de Mola…this is for you. I miss you so much, my baby! Thank you, Patricia Berg, for sharing this! I love you, Pat!!! Mercy Me singing, "Homesick."

9/28/17 bedtime

Goodnight, my beautiful family. Tomorrow will be a very hard day...but by God's grace we will endure. Still can't understand why. Doubt I ever will. But I do know...we will meet again on the other side! Goodnight, Franko. I miss you so much. I love you more! Mom.

9/29/17 Funeral day

I believe I will need people who have gone through the death of a child. I am looking for a support group or something. I got on Google and there seems to be many choices. I will seek the help I need. Don't let Frank Loret de Mola's death cause anyone so much grief that you can't get through another day. He wouldn't want that. Let's allow his death to bring joy and new beginnings for us all. Let us try to find peace and laughter in the memories of his life and put into action what he so beautifully did with his life...HE LIVED...very well.

Later in the day:

Frank Loret de Mola has a new word his friends have created...FRANKtitude. (His girlfriend started the word.)

Think about it! I LOVE this word! I will live with FRANKtitude always! Thank you to all our son's friends for loving him so much! God bless you and love you all the days of your lives!

9/30/17

"God loves those who thank Him even in suffering."

— St. Arnold Janssen

Today...day one again. Woke up at one...Forced myself to not get up. Woke up at three thirty, which has been my usual lately...Forced myself back to sleep. Finally got up at six thirty, realizing this reality. Took a shower...Trying to get a bit back to a routine. Normal life has changed, and eventually there will be a new normal...What that looks like...when that will happen... God will show us. Lead me Lord!

There are so many people to thank for helping to get our Mass for Frank Loret de Mola together! First...I have to thank our beautiful sons, Nick Loret de Mola, Alex Loret de Mola, and David Loret de Mola; his girlfriend, and Fr. Joshua Lickter for the incredible eulogy. I know you pushed Fr. Joyle beyond his boundaries...which is a Frankie thing to do! It was INCREDIBLE! I am so thankful to Nick Tran (Nick), Tony NaRanong, Kay NaRanong, Markus Geissler, Denny, Gerry Lobo, Ernesto D. Agard, Ernesto Agard, Ellen Yee, and the others who sang with the group! My heart felt blessed by the music.

Thank you to the Knights of Columbus friends, Jerry Fong, Philip DeLeon, Lisa from St. Paul, and Lenny Pennissi from St. Paul for the beautiful rosary! I can't thank you enough!

Thank you, Jan'et Blea, for coordinating and making sure everything ran smoothly on Frankie's day. I love you!

Thank you to everyone who came to share this holy day with us. We understand there are different beliefs...ways of thinking...but you allowed Enrique Loret de Mola and I to share our faith with all of you. Being very open minded, we pray hearts and minds were open to our way of celebrating Frank.

We thank God for all of Frank's family of friends who came and became a part of our lives. This part of our lives is our deepest selves...We were made vulnerable to all as we give of our hearts wide open to you.

Jesse Lowther, who flew in from Seattle but lives in Maine; Jeff Norman, who flew in from China; Zhou...we were so happy you were with us! You are all family too!

I also want to thank ALL the family and friends who drove for hours... flew for hours...Sandra Sluss, Phil, Anna, Mark (a.k.a. Mok Lob), Elina Loebe, Joshua Loebe, Sean Grusenmeyer, Mark Grusenmeyer, Brian Grusenmeyer, Liza Grusenmeyer, Marcel, Eric Smith, (who came from England), Mike Morales, and my incredible sisters and Mom, Laura Loebe, Elizabeth Betty Loebe Poffinbarger, Paul Loebe, Ashley Jo Ezell, our Godson Ryan Loebe, Trish Smith who flew in from Dallas, Kathie Loebe, Christina Marie who flew in from Denver...Daniel Poffinbarger and Robert Poffinbarger, and Rosemary Poffinbarger. My heart is rejoicing in the love we share. But more so in the unconditional love you have for our sons. You don't really know them...but family bloodlines are deep and bonding always. We feel blessed!

All my love to all!

Jackie Loebe Loret de Mola

I must add my beautiful niece, Christina Marie, who flew from the Denver area to be with us to give us loving nurse practitioner advice and to be with us through it all. How can I love you more? Forgot her in my thank you post, as I'm sure I did with others...Oh...my cousin David Vasquez! Thank you, Cousin! Love to all!

10/1/17

MEDITATION OF THE DAY

"Prayer, for me, is simply a raising of the heart, a simple glance towards Heaven, an expression of love and gratitude in the midst of trial, as well as in times of joy; in a word, it is something noble and supernatural expanding my soul and uniting it to God. Whenever my soul is so dry that I am incapable of a single good thought, I always say an Our Father or a Hail Mary very slowly, and these prayers alone cheer me up and nourish my soul with divine food."

— St. Therese of Lisieux

I posted this in 2015…Who would have known …? I love you, Nick Loret de Mola, Alex Loret de Mola, David Loret de Mola, and our Heavenly saint, Frank Loret de Mola. I love you beyond words! Thank you for being our sons! The picture says: "Hold him a little longer, rock him a little more. Tell him a little story (you've only told him four). Let him sleep on your shoulder, rejoice in his happy smile. He is only a little boy for such a little while."

Later in the day:
Who is practicing FRANKtitude today? Someone said it's a noun…I think it's a verb…FRANKtitude calls for action…I'm up for it!

Evening of 10/1/17
There was a painting by many in honor of Frank Loret de Mola at Fig Tree. Beautiful evening with beautiful people. Love to all. Can I just say…I miss Franko. Still hard to believe…In time…

10/2/17 my comments and Gus Lloyd:
Thank you, Gus Lloyd, for giving us your reflections on daily Mass readings! I need this one completely!

"A Guardian Angel Prayer"

"Today we celebrate the Feast of the Guardian Angels. In the optional first reading for the feast day from Exodus, we see God telling the people that he is sending an angel before them to lead and guide them. He says that He has given this angel His authority; they must listen to him. In the Gospel reading from Matthew 18, we get the notion of Guardian Angels, when Jesus says that each child has an angel that look upon the face of the heavenly Father.

"Thank God for Guardian Angels! I don't know about you, but my guardian angel has had his hands full more than once. I can think of a few occasions where I would not be alive today were it not for the intercession of my Guardian Angel. And, as a parent, I have an even greater appreciation of Guardian Angels. In fact, every morning, when our kids were still at home, we would say the Guardian Angel prayer with them. Do you know it?

"Angel of God, my guardian dear, to whom God's love commits me here, ever this day be at my side to light, to guard, to rule and guide. Amen." If you've never prayed that prayer before, perhaps today would be a good time to start. Oh, and don't forget to say thanks to your Guardian Angel. Such hard work deserves recognition!

"Father, thank you for giving us a Guardian Angel to watch over us and protect us. May we always be mindful and thankful for them. Amen."

Another Post on 10/2/17
THE WHOLE WORLD NEEDS FRANKTITUDE!

After hearing about the Las Vegas shootings on 10/2/17:
Besides Las Vegas, today has been really rough! First, my love goes out to all who have friends and loved ones in Las Vegas. This is another...unthinkable time. I don't know this person. BUT his evil affects us all! And if it doesn't...then we need to look at you and what you are capable of. Evil is real. Evil happens all around us.

Instead, let's look at the beauty of all who carried the wounded and risked their lives for strangers, family, and friends. Look at the love and prayers being poured out...

We have experienced that first-hand with the death of our third son, Frank Loret de Mola. We have heard the love, felt the love, and received the love of our son from strangers who are now family. We have received the love through hundreds and thousands of prayers offered for our lover boy. We have received love from his life...as we take great comfort in much that has been said on his Facebook page. There are great and wonderful people everywhere! Franko was one of those! Oh God how I miss him. I cry out to God, have mercy...and He has. He took Frank for blessed reasons! His life has given life to someone who needed a heart and was on death's door. His kidneys were put into people who have waited for a perfect match...Frankie was that person for them. His liver was given to save the life of one who needed a transplant. Other parts of Frank are being used for research. That will help with doctors trying to find cures for who knows what.

But today was too real. I hit rock bottom...further than I did at the hospital... I fell asleep on our couch and didn't want to get up...but for Frankie I did. I am in a place in my life where my faith kicks in, and I just go with the flow of the Holy Spirit...I can't do this alone...Henry is on his journey. He is Frank's dad, and his pain if uniquely different from mine. His brothers are in pain, and what they are going through I can't imagine because I still have all my sisters and brothers. So, they are handling this in a way I can't comprehend because he is my baby. My mom is handling this her way, as his only grandparent left. What a load that must be.

Frank's uncles, aunts, cousins, and multitude of friends are all having their unique feelings of loss. Even if family didn't know Frank very well... they feel his loss because we are blood. Our ancestors did a GREAT job of passing on love unconditionally. So, it continues.

I have said to many of his friends that I am sorry for them. His life touched so many from tremendously to in small ways. Everyone believes Frank was their best friend. WHAT a legacy! WOW! We should all be able to leave this world a better place for having been here!

Our sympathy goes out to everyone affected by the life of a man who walked the talk, who lived life more than to its fullest, and who loved like as if he would be gone tomorrow. And it is…but we will go on and on in FRANK-titude…a word created by a friend to describe a positive attitude. I also see it as an action word…BE PEACE…BE LOVE…BE A PEOPLE OF HOPE…BE JOY…BE LAUGHTER…BE A PERSON WHO WHEN YOU DIE PEOPLE WILL REMEMBER AND BECOME BETTER BECAUSE OF YOU!

My love to all! Pray for all of us in our country and our world. Pray for all in Las Vegas. Pray for Frank Loret de Mola!

This mom is finished but waiting for the day I believe I will see him again, as he will give me a cup of Naked Coffee when we meet!

I love you, sons…I love you our heavenly son…

Mom forever…

10/3/17

And…so it shall be…as David Loret de Mola says. But what does that look like now? I want the world to know our sons. How blessed we are to have men of love.

I am waking up most days around three thirty and I know that is a time to just listen and be with God our Father and Our Blessed Mother Mary. How comforted I feel as if their arms are around me. The truth is…I can't do this…whatever this is…without my beliefs. And I am barely present right now to do that…whatever that is.

So I wake up early and pray…a lot…all day. And I find peace in the quiet…candle lit space where I can feel God's presence and His Mother's arms rocking me to allow me to weep. And so it shall be…

Later on 10/3/17

I just want to publicly thank God for answered prayers. He holds us together. He continues guiding us and transforming our lives. Out of the depths of darkness, a luminous star shines to clearly say…"Don't worry"…"I, God, have got you covered!"

Dinner time 10/3/17

Thank you to Carlota Agard for making a FANTASTIC dinner of spaghetti, bread, salad, and lemon cake! Thank you, Ernesto D Agard, for loving our family! Thank you to Nancy Tran, Nick Tran, Jacinth, and Jada Tran for sharing this meal with us. Also…thanks to my Mom, Laura Loebe, and sis Trish Smith for all you've done for us during this extremely difficult time. We love every one of you! I will miss you when you go back to Tucson! But I will see you there! I love you!

10/4/17

Today is the Feast day of St. Francis of Assisi. Here is what Gus Lloyd has as the daily reflection. Today is exactly two weeks since we lost our son, Frank Loret de Mola. The prayer was sung to him in the hospital with Fr. Joshua Lickter singing along. The prayer was the gathering song at his funeral mass. The prayer reflects Frank's life perfectly and will continue if we all can live in FRANKtitude! Thank you, Gus Lloyd and Michelle Lloyd!

"St. Francis' Prayer"

Today we celebrate the Feast of St. Francis of Assisi. So, rather than comment on the Scriptures, I'm going to go a bit out of format for today. Hope you don't mind! If you're not familiar with the Prayer of St. Francis, then today would be a good day to familiarize yourself with it. And if you already know it or know of it, then take a moment to pray for it now. It is a wonderful prayer that can have truly transformative power. Enjoy!

"Lord, make me an instrument of your peace.
Where there is hatred, let me sow love;
where there is injury, pardon;
where there is doubt, faith;
where there is despair, hope;

where there is darkness, light;
and where there is sadness, joy.
O Divine Master, grant that I may not so much seek
to be consoled as to console;
to be understood as to understand;
to be loved as to love.
For it is in giving that we receive;
it is in pardoning that we are pardoned;
and it is in dying that we are born to eternal life. Amen."

10/4/17 more

ST. FRANCIS OF ASSISI...today is his feast day! Another reminder to hold my son, Frank Loret de Mola, close to my heart!

St. Francis (1181-1226) was born in Assisi, Italy, to a wealthy cloth merchant. He was a spoiled child given to pleasure, fine dress, liberal spending, and worldliness. Handsome and courteous, he was a favorite among the nobility. As a chivalrous young knight, he took part in a battle between the Italian city-states and became a prisoner of war in Perugia. After his release he became seriously ill, and while reflecting on his wanton life he had a profound conversion experience. He gave up his frivolous life, cut off his family ties, and embraced a life of extreme penance and poverty in such a dramatic manner that it caused many to think he had gone mad. While praying before a crucifix in the church of San Damiano in Assisi he received his call from Christ to rebuild his Church, which had fallen into ruin. St. Francis followed Christ in a radical manner by patterning his new rule of life after the example of the Apostles in the most literal way possible; he dressed himself as a poor peasant, worked odd jobs for food, and went through the countryside preaching repentance, love of Jesus, and peace. His religious enthusiasm attracted followers, and with these he founded the Order of Friars Minor and the Poor Clares. His Order was approved by the Holy See in 1210 and it grew rapidly. Two years before his death he became the first known saint to receive the stigmata. His holiness was so widely attested that two years after his death the Church proclaimed him a saint. St. Francis of Assisi is the patron of peace, ecology, the environment, animals, Italy, merchants, and families. His feast day is October 4th.

And:

God is my strength.

And a friend from church, fifty years old, died two weeks after Franko.

Sad news...We will miss you so much, Joe Monteagudo. God bless your dad especially. May he rest in peace.

October 5, 2017

"Be one of the small numbers who find the way to life, and enter by the narrow gate into Heaven. Take care not to follow the majority and the common herd, so many of whom are lost. Do not be deceived; there are only two roads: one that leads to life and is narrow; the other that leads to death and is wide. There is no middle way."

— St. Louis de Montfort

I got up at one thirty. Lit a candle. Opened a YouTube prayer, "The Glorious Mysteries Rosary." Comfort replaced sadness as I meditated on Frank Loret de Mola's life. How am I doing? I honestly don't know. I don't want to do this again in my life. But we all know we have an expiration date. A date and time we might not choose. None of us chose this for Frankie. Frankie would never have wanted this either. However, my faith teaches that we are all a part of the communion of saints. I can ask Franko for prayers just like I would ask any of you to pray for me. My strength is from a God who loves me deeply. I have realized and known this since I was four years old. I remember praying at that age. That hasn't changed. If I didn't have my beliefs, I don't know what place my heart would be in. But I DO have a lasting faith in a Lord who will lead me as I follow. Nothing I do now is selfish. It is done with FRANKtitude. I love the thought of FRANKtitude because it allows me to bring our Son with me every step of the day.

My prayer is this, Jesus: Continue Frank's work in me. He was working a Great Plan that only God could have developed in him from a very young age.

I remember when my grandfather Frank Vasquez died. Our Franko was four days from being four years old. We were living in Sterling Heights, Michigan. We found out about Papa's death before the boys went to bed. In the middle of the night I woke up hearing a clicking noise. I realized it was upstairs and one of the boys was clicking his tongue and kind of humming. It was Frankie. When we went upstairs to calm Frank, he said, "He has big hands," and fell back to sleep. Because Franko was Papa's namesake, there was a special relationship. I believe Papa appeared to Frank that night. I found out some time later that when children speak to God, they speak in a tongue language that sounds like clicking. Wow! That was a very holy moment between Franko and God. When I asked him if he remembered that incident, he looked at me as if I was crazy. He never remembered it...I have never forgotten it.

We all have a soul given to us before we were born. I believe that and always will. Frank's soul was perfect, and he used it to make people laugh, cry, reach for deeper meaning to life, give to the poor, love his girlfriend, love his brothers, love his parents and family unconditionally, and love his friends and strangers with care and compassion. He is not and was not a god. He was and is a human being who understood life more than many of us. Through his death, I have learned so much. The ache in my heart will ease, they say. I don't know when that will happen...

Life continues...

Please keep Joe Monteagudo's family in your prayers. Joe's dad Billie helped on the altar for our son Frank Loret de Mola's funeral mass. Joe died yesterday at the age of fifty...His dad and family are in shock. Me too. Joe died exactly two weeks after Franko. May the angels sing him to paradise! You are missed! May he rest in peace. Amen! And Alleluia!

Later on 10/5/17

Anyone who knows me knows I don't like to wait for things. But...I have no choice. I have to wait to see Frank Loret de Mola again, and I know I will someday. By then he won't recognize his old mom. Tears come easily... when will they stop? Even if I want the tears to stop, they kind of heal me. I'm begging God to let Franko hug me or let me see his beautiful smiling face again. I also begged God to let me see him in a dream and then for me to remember the dream. I hope that happens someday...

10/6/17

"In everything, whether it is a thing sensed or a thing known, God Himself is hidden within."

— St. Bonaventure

VERSE OF THE DAY
"There is one body and one Spirit, just as you were called to the one hope of your calling, one Lord, one faith, one baptism, one God and Father of all, who is above all and through all and in all. But each of us was given grace according to the measure of Christ's gift."

—Ephesians 4:4-7

Hi Facebook Family and friends. Just want to say, I love you!

From my Mom on 10/6/17 license plate reading ATT2UDE.
She says:

Today I was on my way to Costco in Tucson, and my angel was right in front of me! Frankie you have such a sense of humor! I am smiling all the way, and I know you're in Heaven enjoying what you have been taught all your life! You are never alone. You are the most giving, forgiving, loving grandson I have in heaven! Grampy probably pulled out his heavenly cribbage board and prays he can win! There is a God, there is a heaven, there is eternity. and one day I will see you and all of my loved ones! Blessed be Jesus, blessed be His holy name! I thank you for FRANKtitude I encountered this day! Love you!

More on 10/6/17

This song is beautiful...It's a prayer, and I could sing it to my Frank Loret de Mola! With a little less twang for sure, but I love it! The song is called "Why Not Me" by Eric Church. Mom posted, and I shared.

More 10/6/17

His girlfriend and her friend Arielle Robbins came over for a few minutes. His girlfriend gave me beautiful surprises! She and Frank Loret de Mola got some religious jewelry, and she wanted me to have it. She gave something for Enrique Loret de Mola...but...ahhh don't tell. GORGEOUS! Thank you.

10/7/17

I received all my documentation for the Holy Land.

When I planned my trip, I had zero idea how much I would need for this trip. God knew...He gave me an opportunity, and I couldn't get it all started fast enough. I thank God for helping me have this time to walk where Jesus walked.

Frank Loret de Mola's death has only enhanced my vision and has given me more peace about going.

All my life I have dreamed of going to Jerusalem. God's timing is perfect! I will take my sons, husband, grandchildren, family, and friends with me in my heart. I am still asking for prayers that one of the men on the trip can put in the wailing wall. Private message me with any prayers you want put in the wailing wall.

Pray for my trip to Tucson, back to Sac, and then off to Tel Aviv…Thank you everyone! Love to all!

Shalom!

10/8/17

Today is blessed. I have no clue what today will bring, but I know it is blessed!

More on 10/8/17

My soul longs for You, Oh Lord. In the depths of my being I never thought I could ache so much. Sure, I have times of laughter and joy. I find joy in Jacob and Emma. I find joy in a pat on my butt from my lover. I find joy in making him eggs for breakfast because my mom told me to…and I wanted to! I find joy in the hugs from our sons and the love in their eyes. I find joy in going to Mass or seeing my beautiful friends. I find joy. I still find joy.

The depth of my joy is so different now. It is felt in my soul…in my heart. It is felt in the lives all around me, especially our family…our sons, Nick Loret de Mola, Alex Loret de Mola, Frank Loret de Mola, and David Loret de Mola; and my husband, Enrique Loret de Mola, whom I could never have made it through this life changing event without! Forty-two years and more…through a God Who can be so misunderstood but Whom I love for carrying us through.

I don't understand this plan. By now I thought I would. I think it wasn't really what God wanted but someone got in the way of God's plan by recklessly driving, and Franko was in the absolute wrong place at the absolute wrong time. And so it shall be. I ask Frank for his prayers because he is so close to the Divine now. He can pray for us like we pray for each other.

Light a candle in the dark...Close your eyes, feel the presence of the holy...Meditate on a time you felt so close to our Son...whether it was during laughter or tears. Maybe you had a few drinks with him and got slap happy...think of that. Maybe you talked so intensely, and he opened your eyes to something you never understood. He did that for me, his Mom... many times...even as a toddler. Then after that...thank heaven...thank our Savior...thank Frank for what he was to you. I do. I always will!

I love St. Augustine! He was the son of St. Monica, who prayed and prayed for her Son to come back from such darkness when he renounced God completely! Here is his reflection:

MEDITATION OF THE DAY
"Now, may our God be our hope. He Who made all things is better than all things. He Who made all beautiful things is more beautiful than all of them. He Who made all mighty things is more mighty than all of them. He Who made all great things is greater than all of them. Learn to love the Creator in His creature, and the maker in what He has made."— Saint Augustine

10/9/17

Just so everyone understands...I am not depressed...It is a sadness...wrenching...and something I have never and hope to never experience again...But we never know. So, I am truly not depressed...I really do understand the difference and for that I am so thankful. I'm allowed to scream, cry, weep, gently cry, etc...and SO ARE YOU! We can do it together in our hearts or when we meet again! Just know...NO ONE NEEDS TO BE "STRONG"... whatever that is, okay? We all are doing this...our way...the only way we know how.

"You can't go to heaven hating somebody. Forgive now. Be compassionate now. Be patient now. Be grateful now. Love Jesus and Mary now. Accept God's will now."

— Mother Angelica

I am a tough cookie...I miss the life we had prior to September 20, 2017... You know...the life I took for granted...The life I merrily rolled along. Life has changed, drastically. So much has happened...I want to turn back time so I can hear your voice, Frank Loret de Mola, one more time...just one more time...But there is a plan far bigger than I understand...Not what I want...but I believe Franko's life will continue in the hearts, minds, and souls of so many...And I truly thank the God I know because I am absolutely sure that Franko is being taken care of and helping God with the needs of us on Earth. I believe I can ask for prayers from Franko to the Father...It is comforting and I feel I then have a deeper connection to my beautiful Son. From birth to life to your sudden loss, to life eternal...you are mine and I am yours forever. Dad, your brothers, your girlfriend, and I miss you so much, my love. Until we meet again...

Today would have been my parents sixty-fourth anniversary. Thinking of you, Mom, Laura Loebe!

Please continue FRANKtitude! Even if it is hard to do daily...you are needed to continue this legacy of love!

10/11/17

Gus Lloyd...Do you hear me or something?...I'm not angry at God, at least not right now... Thank you for this reflection!

"Angry with God"
"In our Gospel reading today from Luke 11, Jesus' disciples ask Him to teach them how to pray. Jesus does. He teaches them the perfect prayer. We know it as the Our Father.

In the first reading from Jonah 4, we read, "Jonah was greatly displeased and became angry that God did not carry out the evil he threatened against Nineveh." This wasn't the only thing that honked Jonah off. Later he gets all atwitter about a plant. And God calls him on it. God reveals Jonah's pettiness, his self-centeredness.

Have you ever been angry with God? I suspect we all have at one time or another. Here's the good news: it's okay. God is big enough to handle it. If you're a parent, your children have been angry with you. I'm sure you were doing what was in their best interest. That doesn't mean they liked it or agreed with it. It's the same with God. He only wants what's best for us. Even if we lash out in anger, he still loves us. That's what a Father does.

Father, help us to see, even in our anger, that you love us and only want what is best for us. Amen."

At Sacramento Airport...going to spend time with family and friends...Not sure if I will hold it together...So what, right? Just know I cry in the weirdest times and places, and I tell strangers about our beautiful son. Strangers hug me...What? Yep. I feel my light has dimmed a little...Will I get that back? Yes, in time. I am using Facebook almost like my diary. I am using it to formulate my thoughts and, in the meantime, I don't want to make others sad. I am venting and sort of talking to myself. Forgive me but thank you for putting up with me. I can say this...I don't know what I would do without my family and friends, especially Enrique Loret de Mola. I love you, Babe! Tucson, here I come, but with a different heart and a renewed soul. FRANKtitude!

First stop before Tucson...in the air again at noon! Thank You God for this safe flight so far!

On the plane...Hugs to all! I love you, Enrique Loret de Mola!

More on 10/11/17

My pseudo-daughter number one, Genny Maze Zawalick, has pictures of November 7, 1995...at the airport as we left Sacramento for New Hampshire...Here they are...Our boys were so little! Genny was at our house ALL THE TIME! She truly was my daughter, and boy could we blend! We learned "Mary, Did You Know?" the week before Christmas, 1994, and she did the harmony...IT WAS AMAZING! I love you Gen! Thank you for sharing!

Pics of leaving Sac in 1995 with Genny the boys and Sheeba.

First picture of David, Genny, Frank and Sheeba. Second picture of Nick, Genny, David, Frank and Alex.

I am in my desert place...Tucson Arizona! A place for comfort. A place for incredible Mexican food and margaritas! But an emptiness envelops me when I get away from laughter and drinks. I think...and dream and think... Is this all real? Did this really happen? Are we all just in a time warp or dream that is awful? I laughed a lot tonight with Mom, Laura Loebe and Patrick, Trish Smith...One margarita only...promise. It took my mind off my beautiful son, Frank Loret de Mola, and Nick Loret de Mola, Alex Loret de Mola, and David Loret de Mola, and my love of my life, Enrique Loret de Mola...even for a couple of hours. But in comes the flood of faces I love so much...his girlfriend...you are right there, my love! Trying to think happy thoughts. Trying to think about life. Trying to think about anything...but it all comes back to Franko. Life is just life. Reality is unfortunately reality. My heart is with my sons and Henry. I love you more today even more than the day you were born! Even more than the day I saw you when I was thirteen. Call me anytime...We can talk, anytime!

I love you!

More 10/11/17

My beautiful Son. I will NEVER EVER stop loving you, my Frank Loret de Mola!

10/12/17

Frank Loret de Mola continuing...On October 24 at 10:30 A.M. Franko will be interred in a mausoleum at Pleasant Grove Cemetery, Elk Grove... Please come and help us in this sending forth a love sign for our beautiful son. It won't be a long ceremony, but it is a way for us to lay him to rest. We love all! All are welcomed. It's a Tuesday and many work or go to school or both. You will be with us in spirit...as you are now. Frank will live on, and he truly is tattooed in all of our hearts.

FRANKtitude forever!

Nothing but love! A pic I cropped of Franko laughing at my sixtieth.

The picture by itself, no words, of Franko, the pic Sandi chose to make for my necklace.

10/13/17

I wake up at one or two thirty now...First thought, Frank Loret de Mola... Why? Why not? I think I heard you call my name, "Mom!," night before last...All I heard was "Mom!" I loved your voice. Please call my name again. I welcome any sign of you, like the white feather I saw inside the airport... so random, but it made me smile. God how I miss you, your smile, your laugh. I'm fine with waking up so early because I can think of you in the quiet. I can thank God for you again and again. I can almost touch you... Please pray for all of us longing and missing you, Son. I love you so much! Amen!

I already said I woke up really early, but I saw my mom was up around three thirty...so I went in her bed and cried and cried as she held me. Enrique Loret de Mola does that for me when I am home. My mom is so strong and loving and AMAZING! THANK YOU, MOM, Laura Loebe, for teaching me constantly how to love with every fiber of my being. I love you...AND... She just made my sis Trish Smith and I, eggs, bacon, and toast at 5:30 A.M.! She never ceases to amaze me! Energizer bunny!

My plan this week was to send thank you cards...I have them...just can't seem to start. Please know I will do it...not sure when. Lots of love, prayers, Masses to be said with Frank Loret de Mola honored...money...flowers and plants and donations to Brain Trauma Foundation. I can't bless everyone enough for all you have done...Oh yes...dinners too! Might be a couple of months...but I will get to them...thank you! As of 5/26/18...still never sent thank you cards.

This Monday night around seven at my mom's house, Michael John Poirier and his wife Mary have so graciously offered to come for a night of healing. If you are interested, please text or private message me to be a part of this amazing night. He and Mary Cook Poirier are coming from Phoenix to share their music ministry with us. Such a huge blessing! Thank you, Michael John, and Mary, so very much!

10/15/17

Going to Mass at 10:45. Tuesday I am getting together with Msgr. Tom Ca-
halane for spiritual counseling and because he has been my friend since I was
thirteen years old. Henry and I fell in love with Msgr. as a HUGE instigator!
Long story...I can't wait to spend time with him and get one or more HUGE
hugs! Henry and I have called him through the years for advice. He has been
a ginormous part of our lives...all of our lives! I look forward to seeing Msgr.
and Fr. Liam Leahy at Our Mother of Sorrows at 10:45 Mass today! Love
to all! Practice FRANKtitude Always!

10/16/17

My beautiful cousin/niece/friend Susan Martinez-Nagele wrote this beautiful
post about Frank Loret de Mola...our incredible loving son. We have incredible loving Sons! Thank you, Susie! I love you!

Susie wrote:

> My cousin Frank Loret de Mola passed away in September. It rat-
> tled our family all over. He was only thirty-three. I was so happy
> to see his grandma, Laura Loebe; his mom, Jackie Loebe Loret de
> Mola; and his Aunt Trish Smith yesterday. Their faith in God has
> kept them so strong. It is amazing for what they went through. We
> were told things about Frank and the impact he left on so many
> friends. Frank had a great attitude and helped so many people rise
> up when they were feeling down. Frank supported people and
> helped push them towards their goals when they thought they
> couldn't do it. These acts and attitude they now call FRANKtitude.
> So, show some FRANKtitude to those you love and to a stranger.

#FRANKtitude

Reflection for today...Another reminder of what my Frank Loret de
Mola was all about:

"We have been called to heal wounds, to unite what has fallen apart, and to bring home those who have lost their way."

— St. Francis of Assisi

More 10/16/17

I know Kathy Lee Gifford can either be loved or not…But she wrote this song about her husband Frank Gifford and I can see that it comes from the depth of her soul.

Thinking I will write a song for our Frank Loret de Mola, maybe, while I'm in Jerusalem…if I am so led.

Amen! Song is called "He Saw Jesus."

Such a blessed night! Thank you, Michael John Poirier, for sharing your deep love and faith! My heart is filled with peace! Thank you, Mary Cook Poirier, for your love of Michael! You both are Christ's work being done on Earth! Thank you, Phil and Anna; Mike Berger and Susan Brossart Berger; Joanie Dymock Tedesco, Trish Smith, Uncle Frank Vasquez and Aunt Jacklyn Vasquez, Sally Barnhart, and my mom, Laura Loebe, for sharing in this night of healing. Frank Loret de Mola, Son, you are the breath I breathe. This whole night was to help us keep you constantly in prayer, but it was also meant for us to stop thinking about your death. Michael's own grandma was murdered in 1990, and he was told that she died once. He kept imagining how it happened, as did others. He was told that when he kept thinking about the way she was killed and imagining how it happened it was as if the act of her death kept happening over and over. It helped me to hear that because I was struggling with the HOW. I can remove that part of my pain. It lightened my load a bit. Yes! I need to think about Frank's life that was so much bigger than his death! Franko did so much, changed so much, loved so much, attained so much, became so much, grew so much, shared so much, and he CONTINUES to do so! That is what his girlfriend called FRANKtitude!

10/17/17

"Our perfection does not consist of doing extraordinary things, but to do the ordinary well."

— St. Gabriel Possenti

Today my morning began with tears. Not tears of a painful heart. Not tears of longing. Not tears of suffering, but tears of thanksgiving for a life well lived. Franko, Frank Loret de Mola, has blessed me, his mom, mother, mommy, ma, with happy memories of his birth, his love, the funny things he said as a little boy, the beautiful smile and incredible hugs he gave, his laughter, his tears, his frustration when I wouldn't listen to him, and his happiness when I began to understand what he was always teaching me. My heart has turned joyful today.

Michael John blessed all who listened and shared last night in my mom's home. The effects of that holy time woke me up feeling peace like I haven't known for several weeks! The grace of the Holy Spirit is what it is called. I wish for all to feel the presence of God in our lives and to know this incredible spiritual journey we are on. Amen!

10/18/17

"Faith and love are like the blind man's guides. They will lead you along a path unknown to you, to the place where God is hidden."

— St. John of the Cross

10/19/17

Wow...emotions just suddenly happen. One minute I am smiling...then five minutes later I'm crying like a baby. I don't know how to navigate this new reality. Yes, I totally rely on God the Father, Jesus His Son, and the Holy

Spirit to hold me through it...as I am allowed time, maybe lots of time to grieve. My relationship with our Blessed Mother is such a huge comfort... but I ache just like she did, and hers was huge compared to mine. I miss Enrique Loret de Mola, as I'm in AZ...He is in deep sorrow...and I think we both feel it is almost too much to bear. So...I will cry. I will weep. I might scream. I will find happiness. But it will be a while. A while. Love to all who are hurting too.

10/20/17

The service for Frank Loret de Mola is this Tuesday the twenty-fourth at 10:30 A.M. at Pleasant Grove Cemetery.

Here is the address:

10232 Pleasant Grove School Road, Elk Grove, CA 95624

It won't last long, but we would love to see everyone there. Our priest, Fr. Felipe, will do the ceremony. One last earthly thing to do for our Son...Just miss him more each day! We love you, Franko!

And...again I see Frank Loret de Mola in this meditation. He lived what St. Ignatius of Loyola spoke of...so long ago.

> "O my God, teach me to be generous, to serve you as you deserve to be served, to give without counting the cost, to fight without fear of being wounded, to work without seeking rest, and to spend myself without expecting any reward, but the knowledge that I am doing your holy will. Amen."
>
> — St. Ignatius of Loyola

Goodnight all! Can't seem to stay awake past nine anymore! Eventually I will be able to. Sleep well! Love to all!

10/22/17

In Love's Embrace...

My friend Michael John Poirier wrote this gorgeous song about his grandmother. She was murdered in 1990 by a stranger. The song overwhelms me this month after Frank Loret de Mola's passing. If you can, go to Michael John Poirier's website called Prayer Breaks, and find "In Love's Embrace" and download it. He wrote this song for his grandma. Here are some of the words. As you read the lyrics, replace Agnes Mary with Frank Anthony and the city of San Antonio with Sacramento...

"In Love's Embrace." Lyrics by Michael John Poirier

"Agnes Mary. It was not your time to go.
How can it be the will of God?
that a troubled soul should take your life?
Agnes Mary, our San Antonio rose.
The fragrance of your constant love still graces us here below.
We know you said let God be the judge
and that's what we are trying to do.
But it's hard not to hate and harder to let go...
So hold us all in heaven's light
and pray we'll have the grace to forgive.
Because we want to join you one day
when tears are all wiped away
and we'll be together again, safe in love's embrace...
Amen."

To our Son, with a love so deep as we continue loving your amazing brothers and each other in your absence. You are not gone...you are just a prayer, a thought, a whisper away. I love all of you but Franko especially today!

Mom

10/23/17 On my way home from Tucson

FRANKtitude in action...even in LA airport! Love it! There was a chalk-board that said, Attitude!

The bottom spot at the cemetery mausoleum is Frank's...How does this ever or will it ever become real? Not any time soon. God gave us this precious Son. He is our peacemaker, and I believe he will always be.

I am home! Thank God for a good trip home.

Tomorrow the twenty-fourth at Pleasant Grove Cemetery...

10232 Pleasant Grove School Rd, Elk Grove, CA 95624

10:30 A.M.
FRANKtitude

10/24/17

It's impossible to think that this life is still going on without our beautiful Son, Frank Loret de Mola...but it in a way it is happening. He is tattooed in my heart. My heart has the shape of love for my Sons to be there with Enrique Loret de Mola and all the family and friends who have made my life worth living. I am changed. I am different now. I understand the sadness and pain that I believe only Christ can get me through. In time...lots of time!

When will I get better...who knows? I'm thankful that I am going to Jerusalem this Sunday. I am going with open arms, an open heart, open eyes, open to all God wants me to learn and experience. Wow! Pray for Franko and be FRANKtitude to all we encounter! Amen!

> TODAY'S MEDITATION:
> "For he will command his angels concerning you to guard you in all your ways. On their hands they will bear you up, so that you will not dash your foot against a stone."
>
> — Psalm 91:11-12

10/25/17

> "Many live like angels in the midst of the world. Why not you?"
>
> — St. Josemaria Escriva

FRANKtitude!

Just got coffee from 18 Grams Coffee and Tea...They sell Naked Coffee thanks to Frank Loret de Mola! Beautiful people. Beautiful stories about our gorgeous Son. My heart is still broken, but now I have a little patch on it. Danny, the owner, is AMAZING! I thank God for Frank's handiwork in this world. He brought so much love in every coffee bean he sold for Chris' company. You can find the store at East Stockton and Elk Grove Blvd. Beautiful store! Have them show you the dove painted on the wall dedicated to Franko. They have a feather painted ready for his girlfriend to write on. It is so incredible! Oh, these tears will never cease. But as I see the joy in the eyes of so many who love my boy…my tears are joy filled too! It's awesome to know Naked Coffee is sold in Elk Grove! LIVE ON, MY LOVE. LIVE ON!

FRANKtitude!

I really miss you, Frank Loret de Mola! But I heard you in my ear whisper…"Hi, Mom!" It was your voice…no doubt! I have a feeling you will let me know you are just a prayer and a thought away! I love you!

10/26/17

> "The goodness of God is the highest object of prayer, and it reaches down to our lowest need. It quickens our soul and gives it life, and makes it grow in grace and virtue."
>
> — St. Julian of Norwich

I am visiting Franko. I am listening to the *Ocean of Mercy* album by Michael John Poirier. While I was in Tucson, millions of tears were put on a cloth and given to me by my beautiful friend, Jill Hermes Kennedy. Never to be washed. I praise You, God the Father, God the Son and God the Holy Spirit, for Your help as I walk through another day of loss and of blessing. Mama Mary, you are with me. You understand the pain…You watched your Son tortured, ridiculed, spat on, stripped, whipped, laughed at, mocked, and crucified as people yelled CRUCIFY HIM! CRUCIFY HIM! But Mary, you saw resurrection. How blessed I am for the gift of your Son! I believe Franko is in your arms and missing us too…as much as we miss him. But Frank has the reality now that we are going to be with him in joy and peace. I praise You, God, for my very strong faith. I would not be getting through this without You, Lord my God. Amen. Alleluia!

Got an iced coffee from 18 Grams! What amazing people! Great place! Please, Elk Grove and beyond…go! Danny and his partner are wonderful people and their little girl is ADORABLE! Thank you for the coffee and yummy scone! I feel Frank Loret de Mola in their place! Thank you!

10/30/17

I love this picture! Fr. Josh and Franko. Fr. Joshua Lickter and Frank became very close friends. Fr. Josh is an Anglican priest who learned of Naked Coffee, and Frank sold the coffee to him. Frank helped Fr. Josh build the business and trained all staff on the fine art of coffee making. Fr. Josh has been a huge blessing. He helped Frank reunite with his spirituality, and Frank helped get the Fig Tree up and ready for business and Sunday Mass said in the store. Makes this mom so happy!

10/27/17

"When you have free moments, go faithfully to prayer. The good God is waiting for you there."

— St. Julie Billiart

10/28/17

Today Enrique Loret de Mola and I leave for San Francisco. I take with me prayers for the Wailing Wall, kisses to be placed throughout Jerusalem, hugs to new friends, love from Henry, Nick Loret de Mola, Alex Loret de Mola, Frank Loret de Mola, and David Loret de Mola. I also carry with me tears and many more tears. These tears are in thanksgiving for my incredible husband of 42.5 years. These tears are thanksgiving for our beautiful sons God created within us, and we have had the awesome task of raising them to find joy in their lives. These tears are also of pain. When I thank God for life, I'm still asking, WHY? That is something I will not really understand...But I accept it, doesn't mean I have to like any bit of it! I cry almost every day. I wake up thinking of our loss. But I find myself giggling at wonderful moments we had with Franko! You are loved, my Son! Your brothers are so loved! I will take you with me to Jerusalem and beyond! You are with me always. All of the family is with me. All of my friends are with me! To say I love you to everyone...Know I truly mean it!

So...I will post pictures...write...and pray a lot for each of you...his girlfriend...you are in my prayers, especially as we share a pain of loss that only a Mom and Frank's love understand.

Let us all stand united in Servitude with FRANKtitude! Amen? AMEN!

Goodnight everyone! For some reason today was tough. Went to Mass in Millbrae and cried. Henry too. Just can't figure out if this really is true or if are we in some stupid movie. I must be so boring right now. I really only think about Frank Loret de Mola most of the time. I grip my hands and shake them and clench my teeth...I don't want anything to ever happen to anyone, and I have an irrational fear of losing any of my family and friends.

I have never ever felt anything like this in my life, and I don't want to do this ever again. Please stay safe everyone! I love you all! I'll be praying for all of you, especially at the women's side of the Wailing Wall. God bless and good night.

10/29/17

Alex Loret de Mola, happy day before your birthday! Dad and I sent you a card yesterday. I hope you get it soon. I love you, Son, more and more each day. Have a wonderful day full of love, laughter, and peace. Hug Allie Criado close and give her a big kiss for us! Have her kiss you back. You will be my first thought as I fly to Tel Aviv! You will turn thirty-six nine hours before you absolutely have to! I love you so much! God bless you and protect you forever!

I thought I would send some happiness on your post! I love you!

More on 10/29/17

Oh how I love them...Franko and Jacob.

Lots of writing…getting so much out…needing this time for healing my heart in many pieces. I am finding the writing is medicine…as is laughter and tears!

Yolie Cox, God bless you tomorrow! I love you, Cousin!

Alex Loret de Mola, Son, God bless you tomorrow on your thirty-sixth birthday…I know I already said something about that…but you are in my heart!

God bless all!

10/30/17 More

On a bus to get to our hotel on the Sea of Galilee! Wow! Getting up early to see the sun rise! I am REALLY here! Thank You, Father God!

Shalom!

It's 3:45 A.M.…Do you know where your children are? I am here, Mom, Laura Loebe! Enrique Loret de Mola…I miss you! But this is truly an opportunity of a lifetime! Our guide has known Gus and Michelle for a while now, and he is amazing already! The history…scripture will come alive even more! The people on this trip are awesome! Can't wait to meet more!

So I bless this day. Soon I will see the sun rising over the Sea of Galilee. Jesus walked on water…Peter tried but began sinking…Remember what we know from the Bible? My faith needs to be strong enough that I don't doubt…but I can question to find…THE WAY! AMEN AND ALLELUIA!

Shalom!

More from 10/30/17 in Jerusalem

Wow, Gus Lloyd! Beautiful! Thank you! I also think of God as my Abba…Daddy!

Michelle Lloyd…can't wait to see what each minute of each day holds. Honored to be with you guys and our amazing group!

"Daddy!"

"What an awesome reading today from Romans 8. St. Paul talks about us being sons and daughters of God. More on that in a sec. In the Gospel reading from Luke 13, Jesus has the audacity to cure a woman on the sabbath, in the synagogue no less! The leader of the synagogue takes Jesus to task for this. But Jesus explains how people, sons and daughters of God, must take precedence over rules. Read his comments for yourself!

"'For those who are led by the Spirit of God are sons of God. For you did not receive a spirit of slavery to fall back into fear, but you received a spirit of adoption, through which we cry, 'Abba, Father!' These words of St. Paul should do so much for us. They should comfort us, helping us to remember that we are God's children. They should embolden us, knowing that there is nothing that we should fear! And they should give us great confidence, knowing that our Father loves us.

"Abba! If translated into English, this word might be 'Daddy!' As Christians, this sets us apart from all other religions. It gives us the assurance that God is not just some authoritarian taskmaster. He is not just some spirit-being off in some other world. He is the One who wants to hold us in his arms, to wrap us with His love. He wants to bounce us on his knee, smother us with kisses and let us know that He will always be there for us, no matter what. Cry out to him now...Abba!

"Father, we thank you for the spirit of adoption you have given, that we may know that we are your children. May we always stay close to you. Amen."

11/1/17

At the other side of the sea of Galilee...Crying!...We threw a rock into the sea to let go of something...I tried to let go of my sadness...But it didn't go... But sometimes I'm not ready yet. Franko you are walking with me...I feel you here with your old mom...I put my feet into the sea of Galilee for you...

The rock I threw in was different from any others...lots of color! Lots of you, Son. I love you!

My roomie took pictures of me singing today. A very God-Moment! Brian, a volunteer at the Magdala center, asked if anyone could sing because the acoustics in the room were incredible. I've been the "music person" for Mass and people asked me to sing something. I quickly wracked my brain, then suddenly heard. David and wife Bonnie (and they are adorable!) from the Houston area, said...Ave Maria! Before I knew it...there I was in this gorgeous rotunda singing the praises of our Blessed Mother. My roomie/friend Mary Dresel took a couple pics and a video of me. It was truly the Holy Spirit! Thank you, Mary! Mary said she'd post the video. I just love my new sister/friend/roomie!

What a day! Its 11:34 and I am wired! Never could I have imagined what I am feeling. My peace is coming. This is amazing! Everyone should come! We are headed to Jerusalem tomorrow...very early! It will be a 2.5-hour bus ride...I hope to sleep! Our Mass started our day and it was nothing but incredible! The boat ride on the Sea of Galilee was AMAZING! The dinner was incredible! Enrique Loret de Mola...we have to do this together next October with Gus and Michelle and my mom! I know there will be some tough walking...but seriously...you don't have to do everything, and you can rest in the bus while I walk with the group. It is so amazing! I miss you, Babe! I Love you, Babe! Love you, Mom! Going to sleep soon!

Still 11/1/17

On our way to Jerusalem...Leaving Tiberius, the Sea of Galilee...Oh my goodness! I woke up happy! I mean...HAPPY! I feel a lot like Jackie Loebe Loret de Mola again! Wow! I wondered if the espresso I had yesterday... NOT! I am so thankful for God's grace and lots of healing! Wow!

11/3/17

Today was INCREDIBLE! We were at the Church of the Holy Sepulcher by 5:00 A.M.! To say this was healing and miraculous is nothing short of what the FEELING is of being in the presence of a Christ Who is both Divine and Human...No way can I ever explain it! We saw the Washing Stone where Jesus was washed and prepared for burial...Its fragrance remains for centuries. I will take scarves down later today to rub on the stones to keep the fragrance. Then we saw His tomb. He was buried in Joseph of Arimathea's tomb...a rich man who lent his tomb for Jesus' burial. Remember...the stone which covered the tomb revealed an empty tomb...BECAUSE HE IS RISEN FROM THE DEAD! ALLELUIA! Nicodemus and Joseph helped get Jesus down from the cross, and both he and Joseph of Arimathea's are buried in that tomb. We also touched the stone where the cross of Jesus stood...Right on the stone is a large crack from the earthquake that happened at His death! Wow! We had Mass in the tomb. That's another story for another time! JESUS COME ALIVE IN ME...OVER AND OVER AGAIN! Mary Dresel and Marilyn Billinger and so many from Gus and Michelle Lloyd and our pilgrimage... Enjoy!

11/4/17

This has been an amazing day. But it was topped off with a phone call home to Enrique Loret de Mola, Nick Loret de Mola, and Jacob! I'm a bit homesick for my family. Hi David Loret de Mola! You were sleeping! I love you all.

More...from East Jerusalem

"Often, actually very often, God allows his greatest servants, those who are far advanced in grace, to make the most humiliating mistakes. This humbles them in their own eyes and in the eyes of their fellow men."

— St. Louis de Montfort

I will share what happened in the tomb where Jesus was laid as we had Mass...

You need to picture a tomb with two rooms so small that only the priest can be in the tomb of Jesus' burial while saying Mass. There is enough room for two people to go in to touch the spot where Jesus was placed. The Mass can only be twenty-five minutes long, and this tomb is under the control of either Israel or Turkey. The Catholic Church was given permission MANY years ago to have the tomb from 8:00 A.M. to 5:00 P.M... I believe. Someone correct me. I can't exactly remember those details...

Anyway...As the priest goes in first to the cave, all forty-nine of us packed into three very small circles like sardines and formed a circular movement as Mass continued so that two could go in, touch the stone where Jesus laid, and go back up to continue the counter-clockwise movement so two more could touch this powerful holy and tranquil spot. After I came back up...I was begging God...crying uncontrollably for a sign that Franko is in heaven. Now remember how very close we all were standing, and my new friends around me held on to me...comforted me as my tears became a part of their clothing. Mass finished, and we spiraled out of the cave, which I NEVER wanted to leave. Right after leaving, Patrick, one of the pilgrims said...He's in heaven. My sign? Yes...But I didn't realize this sign until I spoke with Deacon and Mary...Then I was almost breathless...and so happy!

Sometimes we don't see the sign of God. Sometimes we don't recognize His voice. Sometimes we don't see the panic in a person we walk by or the depression on someone's face. Sometimes we don't see the love of a spouse because of anger and hurt. Sometimes the signs are all around us to seek and to find the answers to our problems, and they are as close as a prayer to heaven. I say...quit looking for truth in things. Start asking..."who is this Holy Man...this Jesus the Christ?" We all might just have our eyes opened wider to a love greater than any...thing.

So many need our prayers...Children hurt in accidents, one in a semi-coma for three years, another one not able to move or talk but aware of life around, people who are suffering over the loss of a spouse, people with illnesses that are in great need of prayer...and also prayers of thanksgiving for blessings upon blessings while God gets the glory! Prayers for all! Thank you!

11/5/17 in Khartoum Eldad, Israel

Michael John Poirier...your songs have been running through my head...as prayers...

"Here in this desert we can lose track of time. We lose our patience and peace of mind. Some will cry out, Almighty God, why are we stranded in this place where the rivers all run dry? Why are you silent? Where is Your mercy now?" The mercy comes from Him...to us within...Mary Dresel and Marilyn Billinger...for you!

East Jerusalem, Israel

What an incredible day again! Began with seeing Bethesda and the pools. Then we went to the Wailing Wall. What a profound impact this experience is still having on me. Did you know there never was a fence between the men and women at the Wailing Wall? This is a more recent event...but I kind of liked the split only because...well...I wailed.

After the Wall we went to see where King Herod the Great was buried. It was fascinating.

After that we had lunch, then went to see the house of the Blessed Mother, Mary. She was born in a cave. We celebrated a Christmas Mass in November. We sang Christmas carols and all. Seeing where the Blessed Mother was born and then seeing where Jesus was born and so much more made me amazed and overwhelmed.

The night ended with a dinner at a Catholic family's home and sharing about all of our lives. What a joy to meet John and Marianne and their two boys: Robert, ten, and Roger, six. And... guess what? Robert turns eleven on my birthday! Marianne made a birthday cake for Robert and me. So special!

The food was incredible. The company was amazing! We had two of our host families come to visit, and they are famous singers and songwriters, and the host, John, is a music producer. Such great people! Thank you to all! Oh, we played guitars and sang...so much to share...Gotta go to bed!

11/6/17

"Guard against anger. But if it cannot be averted, let it be kept within bounds. For indignation is a terrible incentive to sin. It disorders the mind to such an extent as to leave no room for reason."

— St. Ambrose

11/7/17

On my way to JFK from Tel Aviv! I will miss my new friends but SO ready to get home! Prayers for a safe trip for all!

11/8/17

A candle was lit in the Milk Church in Jerusalem. The church turned milky white when the Blessed Mother nursed Jesus. And I cried...Baby Frank Loret de Mola came to my mind and how I could only nurse him for three weeks. My sorrow over that memory got to me. Doctors made me quit nursing because of his jaundice. Many memories pop up suddenly and take my breath away. Time is my enemy and friend.

I'm in New York! Praise God!

I find I take two steps forward some days and then ten steps back... But for me it is the only way I know how to deal with this foreign death thing from losing Frank Loret de Mola. My heart is really hurting today as I sit in JFK Airport on my way home from Israel. Everyone went their own ways, and I am alone...So are my thoughts...Now it's time to get down and dirty with my healing process and allowing myself all the tears I want. So strangers see me cry...WHO CARES! This isn't about me, it's about losing my beautiful Son. Still too real yet. I think I'm in the worst nightmare of my life. My saving grace has been my faith in the Holy Spirit to move me. My faith is in the power of the prayers I ask of the Blessed Mother. She is my rock and my example. She suffered greatly over the horrible death of her Son, Jesus. I understand even a fraction of her pain. I also know she rejoiced in His resurrection. Some day in years ahead...I will be reunited with our beautiful Son. I completely and totally believe that! Joy is coming!

Still 11/8/17

Just saying...

FRANKtitude!

Back to reality...Henry's been on the phone with the insurance company of the young man who hit Franko. Reality smack dab in our faces! Please pray for the right thing to be done. God's will...

11/9/17

I don't know who I'd be without you, Enrique Loret de Mola! I don't know what life would be like without you! God gave us to each other because He knew we needed each other. He knew we would go through the joys and sorrows together in thanks to the One Who Loves Us Unconditionally! God taught us how to do that for each other! I thank God for You, My Love!

11/10/17

To Nick Loret de Mola, Alex Loret de Mola, David Loret de Mola, and our Frank Loret de Mola...This is for you. I love you even if time has stopped for us, including Enrique Loret de Mola... We can get through this together! I love you all so much! Please stay close...Please stay safe...Please continue loving each other...Please continue to have the best memories and share them with me. I need to hear about your relationship with Franko. I need to hear about him. I love you guys so much!

I visited him yesterday and brought him these pretty flowers. Just want you to know. I'm really struggling. Getting away to AZ and Jerusalem didn't stop my tears, but it's different being home. There is no perfect way to do this thing called love and death...I get that. In time, they say, in time. Okay... if you say so!

I went to see Frank Loret de Mola yesterday. I got home from all my travels thinking it would help. I cry a lot no matter where I am. I also laughed that loud laugh in Jerusalem, and I'm sure I drove all my new friends/family NUTS. But it felt so wonderful! I threw a rock into the Sea of Galilee, and the next morning I woke up so joyful. It was an amazing day. But I came home and Frank's being away had started the pain all over again. Deep pain. I think this is okay...but I will seek some help...a group or a counselor or someone who knows all about this "stranger" who is taking over my body and mind.

I visited Franko yesterday and told him I am so sorry for the mothering I didn't do, the mistakes I made, any hurt I caused him, and I screamed cried it...and when I went back to the car, my phone rang. I almost hung it up, but it was my sister Trish Smith...and we cried hard together. Even though she is in Dallas...she held me on the phone and just let me scream cry...I didn't drive then...I just sat there...stunned...hurting...missing our Son... loving him...wanting him back...OH GOD! I WANT HIM BACK! But that's not the plan now.

I called my church and talked to our pastor and said...I can't be in charge of music. I can't even think of the holidays...I'm sorry, I said. All he said was okay…What can he say? I just can't do the music planning. I just can't be in charge to make sure people show up…I… Just don't want to!

I saw Frank's resting spot yesterday right after morning Mass. I brought him fresh flowers, and I took a silk arrangement to Gayle too…And another day goes by…Again…without My Son…Thank you God for my tears…It is a sign of a divine love!

FRANKtitude
Remember?
Let's live it!
Let's be him!

11/12/17

I am so humbled by all the beautiful birthday wishes! This is definitely a different birthday, but it is awesome because I'm collecting social security beginning in January! Sixty-two is beautiful! Just saying…

11/13/17

Severe meltdown:

I need my Mom, Laura Loebe. I will always need her. She is coming on Friday to stay with us. Thank you, Mom! I love you!

11/14/17

Dale Yamamoto and Kit Mapa Yamamoto gave Henry a book last night called *I Wasn't Ready to say Goodbye*. It is me. Leaving for Arizona and the Holy Lands postponed my grieving. So, if I am distant or don't want to do much, please understand. I won't explain myself because I shouldn't have to. If I feel like crying or screaming, I will. What really bugs me about all of this is I don't feel like playing my guitar. I don't feel like cooking. I don't feel like "getting going." I feel like doing nothing. I am allowed.

Don't worry if I am doing this grieving thing correctly. Evidently, I am. It is my way, in this very foreign place. I will continue wanting to hear from family and friends, but don't be hurt if I am distant or I cry easily. It is what it is right now. Tomorrow might be different. Love to all.

His girlfriend came over, and David Loret de Mola and I watched an old funny movie...*The Three Amigos*! We laughed and it felt good. Thanks! I needed that!

11/15/17

I look at your picture,
I can't breathe.
I look at your picture,
I go back to before...
I look at your picture,
I beg someone to say you will be home.
I look at your picture,
I get a stomachache.
I look at your picture,
I am lonely for a hug hello.
I look at your picture,
I realize you won't be here for Thanksgiving.
I look at your picture,
I can't breathe...and
I wonder when I will.
Can I scream now?
Will you hear me?
Is heaven far?
Can I call you on your cell phone?
Will you answer?

Oh God I hate reality.

Wake me up.

Please!

Tell me in two days all of this will be over!

Two months maybe?

Two years maybe?

Two decades maybe?

Oh my God…it is real.

How do I know this is real?

We received a letter from the fifty-nine-year-old woman who received your liver.

She promised to take good care of you.

She's a wife, mom, and grandma.

Her sixth grandbaby was born the Day After

You became a part of her.

That makes this all too real.

I am so happy for her.

You live on, in a way, through this beautiful woman.

She is so thankful.

You helped people after…

I want you back…is that selfish?

I am your Mom…

My heart aches deep into each valve and vessel.

You are in my thoughts always.

I love you.

I love you.

I miss you, my Son.

11/17/17

My new sister/friend, Mary Dresel, told me she thought Fr. Dave Dwyer was talking about me on the Catholic Channel on Sirius XM. I wasn't able to listen so I got on my phone to see if I could get a repeat show.

I had written to Fr. Dave on Facebook during a live broadcast. He was talking about the upcoming holiday season. I asked him, "How can my family and I get through the season after the loss of our son, thirty-three years old, who just died in September.

I was able to get the channel for one month free because we already have Sirius in our cars. From there I was able to find yesterday's show. Thank you, Mary, for letting me know. It was a wonderful show. I felt blessed that they helped me understand more that I am not crazy or out of bounds on my grief. None of us are. It was a blessed divine appointment. I felt they were speaking to me personally. Thank you, Busted Halo Show, for your help! God bless you always!

I've been trying to read about grief and what I'm going through and what others are or have gone through. This book...even though it is a daily reflection and not a lot to read...impacts me.

I am sharing! Thank you, Kit Mapa Yamamoto and Dale Yamamoto!

11/18/17

Enrique Loret de Mola, Mom (Laura Loebe), his girlfriend, and I went to a Compassionate Friends meeting tonight. Wasn't sure what to expect. But it was truly a blessing. I see we are all in this together. No matter how long ago your child, spouse, friend, family member, or whomever has died...the pain is real and SO MANY of us are hurting. Yet, we are willing to listen and be there for someone who can feel others' pain and love each other through the sadness. I will heal, and I will get better. I may have more difficult days. But it truly helped me to know we have family, friends, and strangers who can help us to a new step in this journey! Thank you! I think all people who have been hurt by a loved one's death would benefit from going to a support group like this.

11/18/17

Jacob: What do you call a Thanksgiving about your uncle?

Us: No, what?

Jacob: A Franksgiving!

Yes…and that's how our day begins! BEAUTIFUL!

11/19/17

Gus Lloyd, I needed this today. Since Frank Loret de Mola…Frank's death I haven't wanted to play my guitar. I will at Mass today. Your reflection woke me up. My Mom, Laura Loebe, is here with me, and she will help me start painting again too. It's a new "talent" I began working on but put it aside for months. Thanks so much, Gus!

Here are Gus' thoughts on today's readings at Mass:

"Sins of Omission"

"Today's first reading from Proverbs talks about a worthy wife. I am blessed to have one myself. In the second reading, St. Paul tells the Thessalonians that they are "children of the light and children of the day." And in the Gospel reading from Matthew 25, Jesus tells the parable of the talents.

"In the parable, the master rewards the two servants who invested their talents and got a return. But the third was punished. Why? Did he lose the master's talent? Did he squander it on women, wine, and song? No. In fact, he returned to the master his original investment! Gee, in today's market, that would be a wonderful thing, wouldn't it? But this wasn't good enough for the master. He expected the servant to actively use the talent he had been given. Interesting that the third servant was punished not for doing something, but for not doing something. God has given us all a talent (at least one) and expects us to use that. Even if we try something and fail, I believe that just the effort pleases

God. What doesn't work is when we bury our talent. When we choose to do nothing. It seems that, when it comes to the gifts that God has given us, sins of omission are greater than sins of commission.

"Father, forgive us for those times when we do not use our talents, for whatever reason. Give us the courage to use our talent in whatever way you see fit. Amen."

Today is Enrique Loret de Mola's birthday! Sixty-six years young! Henry is the love of my life. He is a great father, a terrific Papa, a wonderful husband, a terrific son-in-law, an awesome brother, brother-in-law, friend, co-worker, and human! He is honest and sincere! I have never doubted his love and continue to be amazed at his love for all. He has helped me become a better person, and THAT took a lot of patience...and he is the BEST with patience! I love you so much, and I thank God for you always! Happy Birthday, my Love!

11/20/17

Still working on my Frankish painting...Henry and David said to cut some of his beard. Still looks NOT like Frank Loret de Mola...but I enjoyed trying!

11/23/17

Happy Thanksgiving, everyone! It is a blessed day. I think Thanksgiving has changed for me over the years. It hasn't been about pilgrims and the Mayflower forever for me. It's about Enrique Loret de Mola, my kids, my grands, my beautiful Mom, siblings, aunts, uncles, nieces, nephews, cousins, and their families. It's about my friends who ARE my family. It's about taking time and spending time with those we love. It's about remembering those we've lost who continue to live through our wonderful memories.

God bless all. God continue blessing our world
Jesus, bring us PEACE! PLEASE!
As Jacob said...
HAPPY FRANKSGIVING!
We love you and miss you, Frank Loret de Mola! So much!

More from Thanksgiving 11/23/17

Mom, Laura Loebe, cooked everything! She made the turkey...I only helped a bit. She made sweet potatoes, the best stuffing, green beans, Mac and cheese, an amazing apple pie, and lots of love! I made pumpkin pies, and we all enjoyed everything.

You know, this has been such a hard year for all of us. We had many downs and ups...The grandkids are the ups...and then, Franko. Holidays are tough if you have no one with you while going through the most traumatic thing imaginable. But we have so many people loving us and continually praying for us that this Thanksgiving was truly a blessing. Alex came from Seattle by train and is staying just one night. Thank you, Son! Nick picked him up in the wee hours of the morning today (thank you, Son!) and Al boards a train tomorrow night around midnight to get back.

David has been such a great uncle to Jacob, playing games and spending time with the grands. Dave is my right hand and hugs me extra when most needed! His girlfriend, Franko's love, spent Thanksgiving with us, and I love to see how Emma really takes to her. His girlfriend played with her and really had fun with her! I love the laughter. Thank you, for everything!

Henry is the patriarch of this family, and you are so loved, Enrique Loret de Mola! Thank you for taking such good care of us.

We really do have so much to be thankful for. At Mass this morning, I was able to thank God for Frank's thirty-three years. Do I feel cheated by his sudden death? You better believe I do. But... you know what? When I think of all our Son did in thirty-three years, he really lived more like one hundred years. Each day was full. Each day he was constantly learning and helping and being Frank.

Oh my God, I love him and miss him. I still at times don't believe that we just went through Thanksgiving without even a phone call, but he remains in our hearts. He is my Son and will remain with me forever.

I have heard that every mother continues to have the DNA of each birth in them. I know I do because my love for Nick Loret de Mola, Alex Loret de Mola, David Loret de Mola, and Frank Loret de Mola is deep within every ounce of my being...You are the best gifts God ever gave Dad and I, and I am so very thankful on this day and each day that you call me Mom. Thank you for love! I love you all! Thank you, Mom—Grammy—for dropping everything to come to Sacramento and take care of me. It means more than I can say! Thank you, Henry, for everything! With God's help we will get through all of this, and we have the hope in our faith that our journey will lead us back to Frank and all those we love who have gone before us.

Truly...Happy Thanksgiving!

Nancy Tran, thank you for loving us and stopping by tonight! Carlota Agard, the flan is AMAZING! Thank you!

Goodnight all my family and friends. I am so thankful for all your support. I love you!

11/24/17

"Crosses release us from this world and by doing so bind us to God."

— Blessed Charles de Foucauld

I do believe this with all my heart!

Well...our Alex Loret de Mola...second oldest Son, came in yesterday at 6:15 A.M.! He's leaving tonight at midnight! I love you, Son! Thank you for taking the train, riding for an unbelievable amount of time, and loving us so much!

11/24/17 more

Have to think about FRANKtitude and remember why he deserves to have that word! No, he was far from a saint, but my best friend, Sandi Austin, was in a bad car accident last Friday. She said she asked Frank Loret de Mola for help. She did not ask her Mom, Dad, or brother, who have been gone for a while…No, she asked Franko! The accident was not her fault. It was a brand-new car I helped her buy in Tucson, and she only had it for three months. She asked Frank for help. She didn't remember she had gotten GAP insurance. Then Lo and behold! There it was on her contract. Prayers are working.

More graces being given out because of Frank's intercessory prayers. She was transported to a hospital because she was unconscious. She has been home and, other than soreness, all is good. Thanks be to God. No Frank did not do this himself but through God's help too, Sandi is going to be fine, and she will get another car without worrying about the one that was totaled. Thank you, Son, for your help! I believe it!

11/25/17

I love this picture! Frank Loret de Mola, David Loret de Mola, and Alex Loret de Mola can light up a room!

11/27/17

I begin to cry…even when I go to the bathroom! I know…TMI! But I pray a lot in my alone time. Frank Loret de Mola is on my mind. Fell asleep saying a rosary and crying. Will the sting of his loss ever end? Will I begin anew in time? Yes…in God's and my time. But for now, I need to expect the unexpected tears.

11/28/17

Came to Tahoe with my wonderful Mom and our beautiful friends, Carlota Agard and Ernesto D Agard for a couple of days. Much needed. Thank you, Enrique Loret de Mola, because you know I need mindless time. Fun to be had!

11/29/17

Sometimes, I honestly think Gus Lloyd sees my life! There were many signs pointing to so many experiences in my life. I either didn't want to see them or I was blinded by ignorance of my faith. Thanks, Gus, for another faith moment of growth!

"The Handwriting on the Wall"

"I think that many people are unaware that many common expressions actually originated in the Bible. Today is another example of that. We'll talk about it in a sec. For our Gospel passage today, we're back in Luke 21, with Jesus talking about the end of time. I talk often about how Christianity is not a religion for quitters. Why? Because of Jesus' words at the end of today's reading. "By your perseverance you will secure your lives." Keep the faith, my friend!

"'The handwriting is on the wall.' You've heard that before, right? It means the future has been foretold. All the signs point to the outcome. Did you know that expression originated in the Bible? We find it in today's reading from Daniel 5. King Belshazzar throws a big party and decides to use the vessels stolen from the Jewish temple to drink out of. Suddenly, a giant hand begins writing on the wall of the palace. The king brings in Daniel to interpret the writing. It is not good for the king.

"I think that God gives us signs all the time. Now, they may not be as blatantly obvious as the one he gave the king in today's first reading. But, more often than not, the handwriting is on the wall for us. Now, this expression usually has a negative connotation. But it needn't always be so. When we do the right, perhaps the handwriting on the wall can be positive for us. So, let's do the right!"

"Father, help us to realize that our actions have consequences. Let the handwriting on our wall be positive as we serve you today. Amen."

More 11/29/17

Prayers for a cousin who lost his daughter today. So very sorry!

11/30/17

Just when ya think your Mom is leaving one week earlier...SURPRISE! She is staying longer! Not leaving until the sixteenth! Yipeee!

I think our lives are so different now. It's about Franko being gone, of course. But now I have an emptiness I've never known. I have a longing that is way different from "homesickness." I have a breath that gets caught between inhaling and exhaling that almost is a stop-haling. Is there such a word? I get caught in barely breathing to feeling my heartbeat with every breath. This is mourning again. Welcome to mourning. Not morning, but mourning! I am a morning person, but this type of mourning is unkind. It hits me hard each day when I picture his beautiful eyes. I imagine talking to him with his deeply philosophical dialect that I don't quite understand. His eyes just speak to me saying...it's okay, Mom! I barely understand what I read sometimes...Frank said that to me once...so long ago!

Today I feel like it's been years since I last saw you, when you were so thankful I helped your girlfriend clean your old place...Oh how I wish I could help you again, Son.

Oh my God...for the times I didn't see you, you were in my heart.

For the times I didn't call you, I expected to talk the next day.

For the times we hit rough patches in our relationship, and I thank God our love of you being my son and I your mom kept us pushing forward.

Can you hear me, Son? Can you see me and feel me missing you daily? Please continue praying for us, Franko. I love you and miss your laugh, your smile, your sad puppy eyes, your hugs, your dedication to your entire life. I miss you. That will never stop. I love you, Frank Loret de Mola, my Son!

12/2/17

I can't help but think about my Son, Frank Loret de Mola...he was a GREAT teacher! He never did that for a living, but he did that **for** the living. He could teach coffee to calculus. He could teach love by showing his life in action. He could teach peace, which he believed in wholeheartedly. He could teach compassion because his heart was full of feelings for even a stranger crying while sitting on a bench.

12/3/17

Henry and I got married in St. Francis de Sales church forty-two years ago. This is a reflection from St. Francis de Sales.

"Never be in a hurry; do everything quietly and in a calm spirit. Do not lose your inner peace for anything whatsoever, even if your whole world seems upset."

— St. Francis de Sales

12/5/17

I still can't wrap my head around Frank being gone. I kiss a picture of him and just take a breath as if he can feel my kiss. Still very surreal...I had two good days...in a row. That's a start.

Tears flow when I see his picture or something just comes to my mind about his absence in our lives. I know my faith has helped me to begin healing. I know people must think...STOP TALKING ABOUT IT! But this is like walking in a foreign country without a tour guide. Everything is still beautiful but so scary!

I will get better. If I seem aloof or distant...I am. I want to crawl into bed and stay there, but I force myself to bathe, get dressed, and even do things.

I painted a little today. I also started a process to seek counseling. I will call for an appointment tomorrow. I need to learn to not dwell on certain aspects of missing Franko. Why didn't I call him the day before his accident, when I heard LOUD AND CLEAR, CALL FRANK! Got busy with the grandkids and time got away from me. I want to stop thinking I could have done more to see him more often, like going to the roasting plant and saying hi!

I want to stop seeing him in the hospital...I want to remember all the years but that is hard...I have lost years in my memory. Is that a part of the trauma of losing him?

So a counselor will help me. I am needing to know I will be okay...Well I do know that...but I need steps to take to move forward.

Love to all. Goodnight!

12/6/17

"To use this life well is the pathway through death to everlasting life."

— St. John Almond

Thank you for all your prayers! First appointment for counseling is this Monday evening. Praise God because I am thankful for new beginnings.

12/10/17

VERSE OF THE DAY

"For through the Spirit, by faith, we eagerly wait for the hope of righteousness. For in Christ Jesus...the only thing that counts is faith working through love."

Galatians 5:5-6

11/11/17

This particular meditation blesses me today. I have times when I just can't pray. Saying the name of Jesus is prayer. I knew this but forgot it. When I have difficulty praying, I will say His name. He will understand my weakness.

MEDITATION OF THE DAY

"Little by little, we can make our daily life more and more prayerful, as we are able, over time, to incorporate those suggestions that work with our schedule and that we are ready for spiritually. There is a particular spiritual practice that Francis [de Sales] highly recommends that is possible for all of us: even on those 'impossible' days when we are perhaps unable to undertake our normal spiritual practices, we can stay rooted in prayer by constantly addressing brief prayers to the Lord. These can be acts of love, of adoration, of faith, of hope, of petition, or simply saying the name of Jesus—throughout the course of the day. Francis places a very high value on these simple utterances, traditionally called ejaculatory prayers or aspirations."

— Ralph Martin, p. 135, Fulfillment of all Desire

12/12/17

God opened a new door, but I never thought I'd walk through it...Can I please turn back time to September 19 and call Franko and tell him how much I love him and to drive carefully and to come for dinner? And then I will walk through knowing I would do things so differently...Can I please?

I saw a psychologist yesterday. Great advice. I have a feeling he knew Frank. He said he goes to Naked Lounge. He cried too. With me. I will go again...Thanks for all your prayers!

12/16/17

I just left Mom, Laura Loebe, at the airport. Crying is my middle name. I miss her, and my heart aches. She came to my rescue...She revived me. She helped me focus on other things. She cried with me and laughed hard with me. She enjoyed our family and friends. I just hope she decides to move in with us in the near future! BUT THAT WON'T HAPPEN ANY TIME SOON! I love you Mom! God bless you on your way! You are my angel, Mom!

12/17/17

So, this is the Christmas season...very different from any other Christmas. Just can't stand the fact that one important person of our family will not be physically here. But I believe Frank Loret de Mola will ALWAYS be with us. His wisdom, laughter, puppy eyes, hairy arms, gorgeous smile, huge hugs, caring tone in his voice, and patience of a saint! I think the only time I remember him getting mad and hitting something is when he put a hole in our kitchen wall in our Folsom house. He felt so bad about it. I don't even remember why he did that. So out of character. He isn't here...He isn't here... He isn't here...But I believe I know exactly where he is...heavenly Christmas home. I can imagine him playing with all the kids and showing them how to play cribbage or Texas Hold 'Em. Oh my God, my Lord...I miss him. Can you please bring him back and shock the world? Crazy request? Yes...but I'm asking GOD! Sometimes He answers, "No." I understand that too well now. I accept Your answer, God, but I don't have to like it! I love you, Franko! I miss you! We all do...

12/18/17

This is what I'm doing. Not ready to go to bed. Feeling a bit panicky...feeling so lonely for our Frank Loret de Mola. I just want to see you. It's quiet in the house. I feel God calling me to prayer...but all I can pray is WHY GOD! WHY my beautiful son. I can't help it. My sadness overcame me just suddenly...unexpectedly...

I am taking a few steps back, but tomorrow I will move ahead. I tell myself, Jackie! Its okay to cry and hurt and feel the loss. I say, "But it's almost three months...CAN YOU BELIEVE IT?" When can I stop hurting? The thought of you takes the air out of me, and I want to scream. Not at anyone. I just want to scream...even in my pillow. I keep having to tell myself...HE REALLY IS GONE! But I still want to know why! Is that too much to ask, God? Can you talk to me like you spoke with Moses, Job, or Isaiah? I just want to know...

But that is why I have faith. I believe in the fact that I trust in Frank's eternity of bliss. I trust that God is helping me get through all of this. I can feel Mary, who bore Jesus in her womb, holding me with strong yet gentle arms. I believe Frank misses us like so many, especially his mom and dad. I know his brothers are hurting still, like Henry and I. I know the family is hurting, as is his girlfriend...but I defy logic by believing he could still walk through the front door and kiss and hug me saying, "Hi, Mom!" I know anything is possible...but that's another story. I will go to sleep and pray I remember any pieces of dreams I might have with Franko. I have lived a life of pain and horrible events, but NEVER EVER have I felt this kind of pain. I will feel better tomorrow and still think of my Sons, Nick Loret de Mola, Alex Loret de Mola, David Loret de Mola; our grandchildren, Jacob and Emma; Enrique Loret de Mola, my love; my beautiful Mom, Laura Loebe; all my siblings; so many family members and friends…but foremost…at the very front of my brain…is Frankie. Sorry…just had to write before I sleep. Goodnight all my beautiful family and friends. In the near future I will write about joy. But I will also share my struggles with being a Mom with a broken heart. I'm trying…I'm trying to get through this…One minute at a time…Please, God, help me!

12/20/17

"If you wish to go to extremes, let it be in sweetness, patience, humility and charity."

— St. Philip Neri

Hard time of the year for a lot of people. Hotline 800-273-TALK (8255).

A simple copy and paste might save someone's life.

12/22/17

3 months ago today, our Son, Frank Loret de Mola was taken from us by someone who just didn't understand that there were other people on the road. He made the biggest mistake in life, to kill someone. He didn't know the beautiful man he killed, but in time he will. Enrique Loret de Mola had a very vivid dream last night about Franko. I smiled and then cried hearing the dream. I wished I had dreamt that dream. A few days ago, I felt Franko holding my hand. That same night, Henry had his first dream of Franko as a six or seven year-old.

It's hard to even say he died because he is still very present to us. Others have had experiences with Frank since he's been gone. It is beautiful. To me… it is holy. God gives us those times as a way to touch base with Frank. That's how I believe. It comforts me, even though I cry. Oh my God, I miss him!

Alex Loret de Mola and Allie Criado ARE HERE! Thank You, God, for their safe journey! So happy they are here!

12/24/17

This day started with tears…lots of tears. But those tears are not for nothing. All the boys are here…Emma and Jacob are here, his girlfriend is here, and Papa and I are here. Frank Loret de Mola is here…in our hearts. Life gives us unexpected sadness, but I have to rejoice in the Love we had with Frank Loret de Mola for thirty-three years! I love all of my sons and my babe, Enrique Loret de Mola!

More 12/24/17

Going through lots of old pictures…Wow!

Frank Loret de Mola dressed like Pinnochio and David like Bambi! Party at Grammy's and Grampy's!

12/25/17

"If we approach with faith, we too will see Jesus, for the Eucharistic table takes the place of the crib. Here the Body of the Lord is present, wrapped not in swaddling clothes but in the rays of the Holy Spirit."

— St. John Chrysostom

12/26/17

Merry Christmas, family and friends. We made it through this beautiful celebration of life. Tears for sure...but so thankful we were all together!

Henry and I spent time with Frank Loret de Mola today. We picked up a poinsettia plant and held each other close. Quiet time...Peace filled the air...Thank you, Father God, for our faith that You have our son with your heavenly hosts singing Alleluia! Okay...maybe he's too busy making coffee or teaching a lot of angels how to make the best cup in the heavens!

To say this was tough is an understatement. But by God's grace we arrived at a deeper understanding that we need to truly let God be in charge of our deep mourning and lift us from the pain of missing our beautiful son! Not an hour goes by, Son...You are in our lives forever!

I love you!

If I didn't call people today...it's okay. Just needing time to think and be with all of our kids! Merry Christmas!

Goodnight!

12/26/17 more

Oh that face. Oh, those faces of our Sons. How I love all of you!

How could we have known so much would change in the blink of an eye. But it did. We have remnants of love, playfulness, seriousness; deep, deep thoughts, melancholy glances and pondering eyes. I have eternal love that a mother's heart feels with each beat as it soars into unknown sadness, unwillingly learned so quickly. But a new day comes with a smile and a glimmer of hope for seeing all those who have gone before me.

I wasn't ready...I would never have been ready...EVER. And the way I handle all of this is prayer...lots and lots of prayer, which unites me in some greater understanding with Franko.

So, it is a new reality. Still have to figure out what Henry and I are going to do with all of this. We will wait and see and follow where God leads... Amen.

12/27/17

Yesterday my beautiful friend, Cyndi Ralph Gallegos, came for a visit with her beautiful daughters. Cynthia had bracelets made for Henry, Nick Loret de Mola, Alex Loret de Mola, David Loret de Mola, and me. Here's the bracelet she had made for us...I love you, Cynthia so much! Thank you!

Later in the day...

The FRANKtitude bracelets are ordered. I will give them out. It will be about ten days before I get them. No need to give me a dime...Thanks to Cyndi Ralph Gallegos, who gave five to me and sent me the file to order them. Fifty are on their way! Love to all!

Later again...

This Christmas was so different and so special! We had our sons, grand-kids, Allie Criado and his girlfriend here to share the days with us. My sister Trish Smith gave many of us canvas bags she had embossed with my favorite word now...FRANKtitude. I love it!

My friend and sister, Nancy Tran, and pseudo granddaughter, Jada Tran (Nick and JC too) gave me a beautiful cross with a heart. The heart is engraved on one side with love, peace, joy, and hope. The other side is engraved with my favorite word now...FRANKtitude. So beautiful!

Frank's legacy continues in the hearts and minds of all who loved him, cherished him, called him friend, best friend, partner, brother, grandson, nephew, cousin, business partner, and Son. Let's continue to be FRANKtitude. Thank you, Frank Loret de Mola! Forever...

VERSE OF THE DAY

"In this is love, not that we loved God but that he loved us and sent his Son to be the atoning sacrifice for our sins. Beloved, since God loved us so much, we also ought to love one another. No one has ever seen God; if we love one another, God lives in us, and his love is perfected in us."

— 1 John 4:10-12

12/28/17

"We must always remember that God does everything well, although we may not see the reason of what He does."

— St. Philip Neri

12/30/17

"When we serve the poor and the sick we serve Jesus. We must not fail to help our neighbors, because in them we serve Jesus."

— St. Rose of Lima

Just going to bed...I am meeting up with people I haven't seen in at least nine months or longer. I was just going to bed and I looked at a picture of Frank Loret de Mola on our fridge, and suddenly my breath stopped. Funny how emotions can go all over the place and sometimes even in seconds. Wow! I love you, Franko. I believe you can see us and pray for us. I love you, my sons, Nick Loret de Mola, Alex Loret de Mola, and David Loret de Mola. Sleep well. On to another year soon.

Goodnight!

12/31/17

A very dear friend from our parish passed away this morning. Can we just say...GO AWAY 2017! I AM DONE WITH YOU!

"For prayer is nothing else than being on terms of friendship with God."

— St. Teresa of Avila

1/1/18

"As mariners are guided into port by the shining of a star, so Christians are guided to heaven by Mary."

— Saint Thomas Aquinas

Goodbye 2017! I will NEVER FORGET YOU! But I am so ready to move forward.

Losing Terri Schaub yesterday was just not supposed to happen. Last year was a year of really understanding how quickly we can lose our lives. Reckless driving, health issues, and the complete unexpectedness of our internal clocks stopping leave behind unbelievable grief for those of us to pick up the pieces. More than ever, I realize how important the words of love are. Wake up one morning...and never come through the door again. All too real!

I will make 2018 a year for spiritual growth and love of our sons and family.

2018 will be a year to continue breathing in, slowly, and finding my path in this craziness called life. I will enjoy family, friends, our sons, and Henry so they know how much I need them and we need each other.

God bless 2018! Can this, please, be a year without random acts of violence and make it a year of random acts of kindness and love.

Happy 2018!

I love you!

1/2/18

I post Morning Offerings. This one is truly for all!

"Only in Christ can men and women find answers to the ultimate questions that trouble them. Only in Christ can they fully understand their dignity as persons created and loved by God."

— Pope St. John Paul II

1/3/18

Getting my hair done. Enrique Loret de Mola told me I need to start moving...volunteer or something. So, I got dressed, texted my hair person, and THERE YOU GO! Not hanging in jammies today! Feels good to get out!

1/4/18

Woke up around five today. Going to go do something. Missing Walt and Terry Schaub...Terri, you are in my prayers. I will miss you at Mass! I woke up thinking of you and my Frank Loret de Mola and cried. Too soon, my friend...Way too soon.

You and Walt are pillars in our parish. On Sunday I looked over to see you guys and was in complete shock when Fr. Joyle announced you passed away around 10:00 A.M. Thank you for making me feel special. Thank you for putting up with me in the 1990s. Thank you for supporting me through Frankie's death. You are missed beyond measure. Love you, Terri! May the angels sing you to paradise!

From my friend Mary Dresel to me:

"On my walk today I was reminded that the spirit of our loved ones is always with us. A feather, a penny (heads up of course), and a cardinal that was not posing for close ups today.

1/5/18

Wow...deeply reflective:

> "It is undoubtedly true that each of us, men and women, irresponsible and thoughtless as we often are, hold within our hands the happiness and sorrows of others. We cannot help it or escape from it. The power is in us inalienably almost from birth to death—in us, because we are persons—and we are responsible for the use we make of it. Indeed, so mysterious is this power that the very presence of a person who does not realize his responsibility is often the source of the keenest pain of all... The failure to exercise the power to give happiness to others is not merely negative in its results; it is the source of the most positive suffering of all. Thus there is no escape from the responsibility involved in the possession of this power. Not to use

it where it is due is to destroy all happiness. Strange power, indeed, to be committed to such weak and unworthy hands; yet there could be but one thing worse: that none could interfere with the joys and sorrows of others. We might envy their happiness and pity their sorrows, but we could not help them. It would be a world of isolated individuals wrapped in inviolable selfishness; each must take care of himself and the world must go its way."

— Fr. Basil W. Maturin

I spent last night with Sisters from ACTS. We led music for a retreat a year ago and coined our mini-band...Capo 5! They are amazing people, and I feel so bright today and ALIVE! Yes, I will and can cry...but I am realizing the cloud I was feeling was making way for much needed rain and nutrition from God. Amazing! Please pray for a dear friend who just went through bypass surgery. He is doing well. Also pray for Walt and Terry Schaub and family as they mourn the loss of Terri...as we ALL mourn her loss. But my faith comes from God who made heaven and earth, and He is truly seeing me through, as well as Mary, Mother of God!

1/7/18

"But as for me, I will watch expectantly for the Lord; I will wait for the God of my salvation. MyGod will hear me."

— Micah 7:7

1/8/18

A beautiful thing happened yesterday. The recipient of our son's liver messaged me on Facebook. She wrote on December 21, 2017. I wonder why didn't I see her message until yesterday? God's timing is perfect. Wow!

She is a beautiful woman, and I hope we can meet her one day. She is sincere, will take great care of the part of Frank that now lives through her. And I cry...tears of longing for Franko and tears of great joy for Polly. Frankie was selfless by donating his final gift of love to others who can continue to survive and live life to their fullest. God, I praise you for this incredible woman who truly is thankful for the gift of continued life because of our son. Bless her body, Jesus, and grant her a life of abundance and peace. Amen!

Polly, thank you for reaching out. Love to everyone on this blessed day!

Rough day off and on. I am fine. Rough days prove my humanity, which can stink, or I can embrace it and go with it. I choose to embrace.

1/9/18

Yes...amid all the chaos and controversy in our world...in spite of loss...we really do have a wonderful world!

Good Morning my beautiful family and family of friends! Wow! I am overwhelmed! Frank Loret de Mola's liver recipient gave me permission to share her name with all. She is the most beautiful woman and so very generous to allow all of us to be a part of her Facebook life. And eventually, and hopefully in the not too distant future, Enrique Loret de Mola, a.k.a. Henry, will meet her. I am proud and humbled to share Polly Bleavins with you. I am in awe that God gave Franko to her and back to us. Love hard, live FRANKtitude, and thank God for the gifts our son so generously gave! Thank you, Polly! Thank you! Much love to you!

> "Christ made my soul beautiful with the jewels of grace and virtue. I belong to Him whom the angels serve."
>
> – St. Agnes

1/11/18

Wow! Gus Lloyd's words today really touch me. Thank You Father for people in our lives that share their faith and love of You. May we be open to learning!

"Lessons from Adversity"

"When we choose to follow God, life ain't always a bed of roses. I'm sure you've experienced this. Challenges still come our way. People we love get sick and die. Certainly, there are times where we experience illness, pain, broken relationships, terrible defeats. It's nothing new.

In our first reading today from 1 Samuel 4, the Israelite army is badly beaten by the Philistines. The children of Israel ask, 'Why has the LORD permitted us to be defeated today by the Philistines?' They then go fetch the ark of the LORD and bring it into battle with them, obviously thinking that this would give them victory. It didn't. In fact, the Philistines captured the Ark, killed thirty thousand men and killed Eli's sons, Hophni and Phinehas.

"There's an age-old question: Why do bad things happen to good people? The Israelites were probably thinking that very thought. Now, I don't pretend to know the mind of God, but I think one of the reasons why God allows us to experience defeat is to teach us lessons. Humility is always a big one for me. We can complain and whine when adversity comes our way. Truth be told, that's probably the natural reaction. Or we can ask God not why he allowed us to be defeated, but what he wishes us to learn from our defeat.

"Father, we're sorry for the times we whine and complain and question you when we experience defeat. Help us to use all that happens to us, positive and negative, as a learning experience. Amen."

1/11/18

VERSE OF THE DAY

"Let your light shine before men in such a way that they may see your good works, and glorify your Father who is in heaven."

— Matthew 5:16

Woke up a bit after 5:00 A.M. I haven't done that since Frank Loret de Mola, well you know... Was able to pray and just think. Love the time with me, God, and our Blessed Mother!

1/14/18

"If the heart wanders or is distracted, bring it back to the point quite gently and replace it tenderly in its Master's presence. And even if you did nothing during the whole of your hour but bring your heart back and place it again in Our Lord's presence, though it went away every time you brought it back, your hour would be very well employed."

— St. Francis de Sales

1/15/18

Amazing few days with friends I love from Michigan.

We met Kathy Zalar, Lori Zalar Ruzza, Deborah Zalar Ballios, and Lisa Gray sometime in the late 1980s. Friendship and love began immediately, and we started a singing group for St. Mathias parish in Sterling Heights, Michigan.

They are the salt of the earth people. They are family. Friends who have become OUR family know exactly what I mean. This encompasses all of you who have passed through our lives, my life, and remain a part...no matter how far away you are.

I have been blessed knowing my Michigan family for all these years. I have loved the parents of Lori and Debbie. Rich and Kathy have been married almost fifty years. Rich's mother was adorable and feisty, and her sense of humor could undo even the best comics of our time.

We have laughed until the bathroom wasn't close enough and cried until our eyes dried up. These are the blessings and gifts given in life. If you know people like my friends, NEVER let go. Even their friends became my family too!

You see, life is instantaneous. One day we are here growing up and running the gamut of good and bad. Then we pause, close our eyes for what seems like just a second, and it is all gone.

I remember Frank Loret de Mola, a.k.a. Franko, asking me, "What is the purpose of life?" I remember being stunned that a six or maybe seven-year-old would ask me that. I almost didn't know what to say. But I remember saying something to him about we are here to love and be loved. But now that I have lived this long, I understand more. This life, for me, is to give love, then thank God for love, to meet love, then thank God for love, to be loved, then thank God for love. How could Henry, the boys, and I have made it through so many moves? Because we did it WITH Love...God... gracing us through each step of the way, through the beauty of each person we have met, and through the sorrow which comes when there is LOVE.

THANK YOU, my beautiful friends, for loving us. For loving me! Thank you Lisa, Kathy, Lori, and Deb for SHOWING love. Our bond goes beyond explanation, and no explanation is needed because we know who gave us to each other. Because of our holy spiritual connection, we know there will be more times of laughter and tears in the future. Thank you for loving our family so much and for coming to support us in our saddest of times. Because of our friends, our tears become joy-filled with love. I love you!

1/15/18

Today something so beautiful happened again in our family. Today one of Frank's kidney recipients reached out to me and gave me permission to share her name with all. Meet Gina Pak Dela Cruz. She is a beautiful woman who knows our heartache over losing Frank Loret de Mola...Franko...Frankie. May God continue your healing and many people will possibly get in touch with you too. Polly knows some of that now. Love to you and thank you!

TODAY'S MEDITATION

"And above all, be on your guard not to want to get anything done by force, because God has given free will to everyone and wants to force no one, but only proposes, invites and counsels."

— St. Angela Merici

1/18/17

"Humility, obedience, meekness, and love are the virtues that shine through the Cross and the Blessed Sacrament of the Altar. O my Jesus, help me imitate you!"

– St. Anthony Mary Claret

1/19/18

From Mark Hart:

"...for You knit me in my mother's womb."

— Psalm 139:13

"Every good and perfect gift is from above." -

— James 1:17

"The life of the body is the soul; the life of the soul is God."

— St. Anthony of Padua

1/20/18

Today is four months since our lives took a turn toward the unexpected. I am still finding days of disbelief and sadness. I am sad that each month I find myself crying around the twentieth and having a hard time, especially at night.

Last night I said, "I'm your mom! I'm supposed to save you, Son! I'm your Mom...I should rescue you. I'm your Mom...I want to hold you until you are better. But I realize...you are better. You are perfect. You are missing us as much as we miss you, but you are holding a special place for us...someday. We all are hurting, in our own ways, in our own time.

I miss you, Frank Loret de Mola, more each day. I love you to heaven and back. I have heard you say, "Hi, Mom." Please say it again and again. What keeps me hopeful are the beautiful women now in our lives because of you, Son. They are amazing! But the truth is...you still aren't here and that is the reality that I face. That is the reality we all face. Your beautiful soul is deep and continues to live. I will always believe that there is and was a higher purpose in mind for you, whether on earth or in heaven. I love you!

Your Mom, forever!

1/21/18

I know I have opinions and beliefs that some people are very uncomfortable with. I try so hard to not judge (our sons have helped me with loving and acceptance) but I fall short of God's plan. That's where repentance comes in. Gus Lloyd speaks simply about today's reading. He helps me put scripture in my understanding of my daily life!

"The Call to Repent"

"The theme that runs through our readings today is repentance. In the first reading, Jonah goes through the great city of Nineveh and tells the people the time has come to repent of their wicked ways. In the second reading, St. Paul tells the Corinthians how they need to change their behavior. And in the Gospel reading from Mark 1, Jesus begins His public ministry with a call to repentance. These readings definitely strike a chord with me.

"You see, almost every day, I get called on the carpet by someone for being "judgmental." This is because I talk about sin. I remind people about things that, according to the teachings of the Church, are against the will of God. Therefore, this makes me 'judgmental.' I wonder if the people of Nineveh felt the same way about Jonah. I can hear them now, 'Don't be so judgmental, Jonah! Haven't you ever sinned? Who the heck are you to tell us that what we're doing is wrong!? That's between us and God! Go away, you judgmental bigot, and look after your own sins!' I'm sure many probably felt that way about Jesus.

"The body of Christ is made up of many different parts. Each of us has a particular ministry to carry out. Part of my ministry is to teach. And sometimes that means telling people that certain things are sinful. I hope you'll agree that we sometimes need to be reminded what God expects of us. That thought makes me pretty unpopular at times. But that's okay. Hopefully, I'm just being faithful to what God has called me to do. There are days when I feel much like Jonah…'Sorry, God, you got the wrong guy!' And every fiber of my being wants to turn tail and run. But I realize that I'm not alone. Don't we all feel that way now and again?

"Father, thank you for calling us to ministry, whatever that ministry is for each of us. Help us to remain faithful to your call to repent. Amen."

VERSE OF THE DAY

"Have I not commanded you? Be strong and of good courage; be not frightened, neither be dismayed; for the Lord your God is with you wherever you go."

— Joshua 1:9

1/22/18

I was having a really tearful morning, especially in my car on the way to see my new doctor. I miss Frank Loret de Mola...my Son...my Franko. Four months today, and he is right with me. I talk to him a lot and ask him to pray for us. I believe he is good with that!

So...my heart was super heavy these past five days, but my new doctor's M.A. hugged me and at the end of my appointment, my new doctor hugged me! What a connection immediately!

I got home, and no more than five minutes later, the doorbell rang. A woman was holding an Edible Arrangement for us. I know I've shared a lot about my grief with losing our baby, but I couldn't imagine who sent this. I brought the huge arrangement in and looked at the card...Gina, one of Frank's recipients of his kidney, had sent it. She knew I was hurting. I immediately thank God for Gina and Polly, and I am still in awe of the love we all share! Blessings abound! Thank you, Gina Pak Dela Cruz, for this gift! I am humbled and so thankful! Love you!

1/24/18

I have had a really unexpectedly HARD week! Is this how it goes?

> Tears cascading
> Flooding my face
> Stuffing my nose
> I can't breathe
> My love is holding this fetal woman
> Rubbing my back
> Sobs drowning the silence of the 4:00 A.M. day
> I am paralyzed
> In thoughts
> Of a baby born thirty-three years ago
> Of a four year-old

With a smile, a light from his face
Oh how I long for you
I understand the depth
Of sorrow
Of longing
If I could just take your place
Or remove this repeating dream
Of sadness…Of sadness…Of sadness

1/24/18

Oh my Son, Franko, Frank Loret de Mola, this daily reflection is YOU!
Words this Mom needed so much! Thank You, My God!

"A tree is known by its fruit; a man by his deeds. A good deed is
never lost; he who sows courtesy reaps friendship, and he who
plants kindness gathers love."

— St. Basil the Great

On Monday I went to Kaiser for my first appointment with my new doctor.
VERY impressed with Kaiser! I took my meds with me in my FRANKtitude
bag my sis Trish Smith made for Christmas for many family members. That
was Monday. Last night I wanted to put something in the bag, and I searched
high and low for it. After searching…I thought…*Did I leave it at Kaiser?*

I called an eight hundred number. After four phone transfers, I got in touch
with security at the facility and SURE ENOUGH! THEY HAD IT! The security
guard said…"So are you coming over in the morning?" I said, "Is 8:00 A.M.
too early? We will give it to you tomorrow around eight-ish…okay? I felt incredible…My FRANKtitude bag was lost, but has now been found! Alleluia!

Tears of joy fell as I spoke with Chris the security angel this morning, a
few minutes ago, and I gave him a FRANKtitude bracelet and told him about

Frank Loret de Mola. No, I will never forget you, my Son! And more and more people will be blessed having heard your name and your story. A life well spent, albeit too soon gone.

I am sitting in my car at Kaiser's parking lot...touched by this moment and listening to my Jesus music on Sirius XM. I praise You, God, even in peculiar places. I lift up all who are in need of prayers, as my car has become my sanctuary today! Amen!

Later in the evening of 1/24/18

Henry and I went to Fig Tree tonight. It was amazing! So wonderful to see Fr. Joshua Lickter and Rachel Lickter! Thank you for being a part of our family! You are amazing people, and our son, Frank Loret de Mola, was blessed to know you. Yours was a divine appointment.

Fig Tree is everything and more! The Holy Spirit was palpable tonight! The talent was AMAZING! Thank you for being a shining star in the north for Sacramento! God bless you and let's do this every year for fifty more at least!

1/25/18

"We find rest in those we love, and we provide a resting place for those who love us."

— St. Bernard of Clairvaux

VERSE OF THE DAY

"Peace I leave with you; my peace I give to you; not as the world gives do I give to you. Let not your hearts be troubled, neither let them be afraid."

— John 14:27

1/26/18

"Listen with the ear of your heart."

— St. Benedict of Nursia

1/27/17

Sometimes I meet people who think about life in a completely opposite way from me. I learn. Hopefully they learn. I believe I can accept and not be anything like you. I hope I get similar acceptance.

I am going to take time off of social media...I will still be reachable on messenger.

Hugs and bye!

2/1/18

Hi, just an update...We are doing fine. Met the D.A., not much to say. This will take a lot of time. Arraignment is tomorrow for the person who drove recklessly and accidently killed our son. It will be quick...Pray for us.

New info...Stress is running high. My heart races. God is guiding this process. He has to...I'm fried.

Love to all. Thank you for your prayers.

2/2/18

Arraignment postponed until Feb. 22. God bless this process...Saw the young man and can put a face to his name now. Okay...what now? So what? Heart racing...Blood pressure was up...All I could do was pray for protection for everything we were hearing from other cases. Easy to be in shock, afraid, saddened by society, sad we can't live in peace without fear of harm... but this is the world.

I asked St. Michael for protection while in the courtroom. I prayed for us with us. I prayed for him...So awful that all of this has to be happening. I won't be there for the arraignment. It's okay. He hasn't even been booked. He will be booked tomorrow. WHAT? I don't get that...but I don't have to.

Remember Jackie...in God's hand. Gently walk through the process... Be love...Be FRANKtitude...WWFD...what would Frank Loret de Mola do? See all people as Christ. Live love. Live peace. Live...

Okay...so I'm sort of back on. I miss my Facebook life. I love reading things...about you and others, and it's a place for me to be...sometimes just be...sometimes not...

Hi!

May I just say... I WANT TO SCREAM! But I would scare Henry and David! Just thinking about this week. It is surreal. Completely...My life is just a blur these past four-plus months. I am me...but who IS that? I know this will be all over and finalized...just someone wake me up when it's over! I mean...oh my goodness...I mean...just not real completely yet. And I reach for love...everywhere!

2/3/18

Just left our youngest son, David Loret de Mola...And yes...at the train station...going to do some gigs in many places. So happy for him. Worried mom...and dad...Go with God. Angels surround David and bless him as he blesses so many with his abundantly holy gifts of words, laughter, peace, hugs, and so much love!

Can't sleep. As his girlfriend said, this week broke me too. I came downstairs and saw Sandi Austin; my wonderful friend had answered a question for me. Then I saw that Gus Lloyd had sent his morning reflection on the readings from today's Mass...The reflection is on Wisdom. Wow! I will post it...You read it...please...and understand THIS is what I seek. This is what we all should seek. I want to understand what it is we need to know what is right. I am crying harder than I have, trying to seek what is the will of a God who loves us ALL...EQUALLY...SAINT AND SINNER...GOOD AND BAD...RIGHTEOUS AND INDIGNANT...

WHO THE HELL AM I TO JUDGE? WHO?

I need to lay this at the cross, like I thought I had...Why am I taking it back? Why am I? Why?...WHY! Oh God I seek You! I cry out to YOU! Be with me! Give me WISDOM TO DO YOUR WILL!

Gus Lloyd:

"Asking for Wisdom"

"In today's first reading from 1 Kings 3, we meet Solomon. Solomon's father, David, had just died. The son had ascended to the throne of Israel. More in a moment. In our Gospel reading from Mark 6, we see great crowds coming to find Jesus. 'His heart was moved with pity for them, for they were like sheep without a shepherd.'

"Solomon is known as the model of wisdom. But he didn't get that way on his own. It wasn't his long life or many experiences that gave him wisdom. You see, when he took the throne of his father, David, he was a very young man, probably just a teen. In our first reading today, God tells Solomon that he can have anything he wants. Just ask. Are you serious, Lord? Anything? So, what did Solomon ask for? 'Give your servant an understanding heart to judge your people and to distinguish right from wrong.' Wow! Solomon, a mere youth, can have anything he asks for. And he asks for wisdom. Can you imagine? God was pretty impressed. So, He gave him more wisdom than anyone ever on the planet. I'm a big believer that the beginning of wisdom is simply asking God for wisdom. Worked for Solomon.

"Father, give us wisdom. Help us to know your will, to know your heart. Amen."

Wow! My quiet time is just perfect today...Who needs sleep? I hear quiet. I feel quiet. I smell quiet.

More 2/3/18

I receive emails regarding faith, scripture, reflections, and saint stories, but this morning has been SO incredible. Glad I couldn't sleep because...I'm listening loudly and clearly...Jackie Loebe Loret de Mola...be still...Give God the reigns...Let GO!!!

Here's today's Meditation:

> "Undertake courageously great tasks for God's glory, to the extent that He'll give you power and grace for this purpose. Even though you can do nothing on your own, you can do all things in Him. His help will never fail you if you have confidence in His goodness. Place your entire physical and spiritual welfare in His hands. Abandon to the fatherly concern of His divine providence every care for your health, reputation, property, and business; for those near to you; for your past sins; for your soul's progress in virtue and love of Him; for your life, death, and especially your salvation and eternity—in a word, all your cares. Rest in the assurance that in His pure goodness, He'll watch with particular tenderness over all your responsibilities and cares, arranging all things for the greatest good."
>
> — St. John Eudes, p. 363, *A Year with the Saints*

W O W. W O W. W O W

I praise You, my Savior! Thank you for waking me to listen in YOUR quiet...Amen!

Shhhh...Thank You...Shhhh...Wow...Jackie...listen...

More 2/3/18

I love my husband, Enrique Loret de Mola! He said he wants me to still go on Feb. 12. I will. The stress from this week took a huge toll on me. I need my Tucson home. I know many people have probably gone through something like this…Emotions are unpredictable. Henry helps stabilize me and helps me realize better what I need and don't need. No matter how strong I am, I have a breaking point.

More 2/3/18

I just spoke to my high school best friend, Nancy Cacioppo-Bonner, whose son was a police officer in Glendale, Arizona. Eleven years ago, this month, he was shot and killed at a routine traffic stop. He had already served in Afghanistan…He was twenty-three years old. She emailed me this morning asking me if I was okay. She lives in the Glendale, AZ area. I called her immediately, and we cried and cried. Our losses are similar…Our beautiful sons are gone. Her son was murdered, and His MURDERER is now on death row.

We spoke about similarities and HUGE differences. Neither of our sons, our Frank Loret de Mola or her son, Anthony "Tony" Holly, knew the day would be their last. She truly understands what we are going through and why we want leniency. Completely different circumstances.

And I stand firm…I will NEVER change my mind…No civil lawsuit, no blood money, will EVER bring our beautiful son back to us. However, the stretch of highway Frank was killed on is widely known as "blood alley." CALTrans is well aware of four people being killed in 2017 ALONE! I heard that CALTrans knows of the problem. For there to be a NAME given to this stretch of road…it's disgusting! SOMETHING MUST BE DONE! There have been MANY complaints about Highway 120…NOTHING has been DONE!

My prayers go out for all of us involved who love Franko and for the other side of this issue who need our prayers as well. May God bless and heal all pain in time, and may God bring the right avenues opened to stop the deaths on Highway 120! Pray for the correct people to come into our lives to get this started! It will take time, and it won't happen for a while…Give me time…Let me get strong again…and I will begin looking for info! AMEN!

Having a great day with our grands. Can I say, they are the medicine of my heart. I am calmed by the noise and laughter. Sounds of joy in high pitches and made up words…Ah so lovely and loving.

And more
Wonder if I will sleep.

Nicolas wrote a gorgeous post on Facebook and it took my breath away. Our sons write not with pens or pencils, but with their hearts. Frank Loret de Mola was a writer, an incredible writer. For our sons to quote each other's words because those words affected them deeply is to know the love of their brotherhood in a way that I can only look on or read about in awe.

When I say our sons continually teach me…it is no joke. How I missed opportunities to know their thoughts through their heart-pens.

Nighttime 2/3/18
I will pray myself to sleep tonight with my childhood prayer my mom taught me…It's yours now to share with your kids, as I have with Jacob…not often enough.

Angel of God, my Guardian dear, to whom God's love commits me here, ever this day be at my side, to light and guard, to rule and guide. Amen.

2/4/18
"When one has nothing more to lose, the heart is inaccessible to fear."

— St. Théodore Guérin

2/5/18

Wow...pondering truth...pondering my life and *why do I feel people's pain?*

"A man threw away everything he had—his right to speak freely, his communion with God, his time in Paradise, his unclouded life—and went out naked, like a survivor from a shipwreck. But God received him and immediately clothed him, and taking him by the hand gradually led him to heaven. And yet the shipwreck was quite unforgivable. For this tempest was entirely due, not to the force of the winds, but to the carelessness of the sailor. Yet God did not look at this, but had compassion for such a great disaster...Why? Because, when no sadness or care or labor or toil or countless waves of desire assaulted our nature, it was overturned and fell. And just as criminals who sail the sea often drill through the ship with a small iron tool, and let the whole sea into the ship from below, so when the devil saw the ship of Adam (by which I mean his soul) filled with many good things, he came and drilled through it with his voice alone, as if it were an iron tool, and stole all his wealth and sank the ship itself. But God made the gain greater than the loss, and brought our nature to the royal throne."

— St. John Chrysostom,
p. 19, *A Year with the Church Fathers*

2/6/18

VERSE OF THE DAY

"My little children, I am writing these things to you so that you may not sin. But if anyone does sin, we have an advocate with the Father, Jesus Christ the righteous; and he is the atoning sacrifice for our sins, and not for ours only but also for the sins of the whole world."

— 1 John 2:1-2

Thinking about my family…Our sons and grandson…missing us…terribly…
Still just don't get it…

More 2/6/18
Just feel like saying hi to Gina Pak Dela Cruz and Polly Bleavins. Hugs to you!

2/7/18
"Be who God meant you to be and you will set the world on fire."

— St. Catherine of Siena

Today the world lost a beautiful soul. I didn't know Shelley Shepard well, but what I knew was amazing!

I met Shelley through my oldest friend, Pamela Pulido, around 1974 or so. Shelley and Pam were sorority sisters at the University of Arizona Chi Omega…in Tucson. I know Sandi Austin spent a lot of time with them at the U of A and had a friendship with Shelley too. My heart aches for you both.

Shelley, Sandi, Maria, and I took a trip to Disneyland together last year. I drove down, and Shelley drove back with me to Sacramento. We had an amazing ride back. She and I talked each other's ears off! I won't ever forget our hours together.

This past September, our son, Frank Loret de Mola was in a car accident and passed away. Shelley texted me EVERY SINGLE DAY for a couple of weeks always offering her listening ears to help me. I was blessed by her love.

One weekend Shelley spent the night at our home, and Nancy Tran, Jada Tran, Shelley, and I went to a Mediterranean or Greek restaurant and then out to see *My Big Fat Greek Wedding 2*. We had a slumber party and enjoyed each other's company.

Life can be so unfair. But with faith and trust…we can endure all things…through Christ who strengthens us.

I will miss you, Shelley. Thank you for helping me through the hardest days. Go meet Frankie. You will love him!

Love you, my friend.

Tears…tears…some of grief and a lot of joy. Becoming friends with two of Frank Loret deMola's donor recipients—one of his liver and one of his kidneys—has been AMAZING! God blessed our family with Polly Bleavins, liver recipient, and Gina Pak Dela Cruz, kidney recipient. The thing that brings joy is the many people who know Gina and Polly who now know our son and all who love him. Your friends/family are amazing like you, Polly and Gina! Thank you. It is with a joyful heart we have now extended our family to more people we don't yet know. WOW! This is what Frank wanted! He CHOSE donation, and he is now being honored by the lives touched through his generosity! WOW! I praise You, God, for all Your works are wonderful! Amen!

More 2/7/18

Sometimes I want only happiness sewn…Sometimes that's not how the journey goes.

I am shattered but not defeated. I cry so easily, and at times I scream in my pillow.

I don't always understand the real pain in loss…because I don't want to know it.

I take each moment in baby steps, and if I leap…let me. It's rare to leap while being pinned down to sadness.

I will rise to new heights and reach the peace within in time. Until then I will continue on this journey of this tapestry called life.

2/8/18

"If a tiny spark of God's love already burns within you, do not expose it to the wind, for it may get blown out…Stay quiet with God. Do not spend your time in useless chatter…Do not give yourself to others so completely that you have nothing left for yourself."

— St. Charles Borromeo

2/10/18

VERSE OF THE DAY

"For the message about the cross is foolishness to those who are perishing, but to us who are being saved it is the power of God."

— 1 Corinthians 1:18

2/12/18

"Fix your minds on the passion of our Lord Jesus Christ. Inflamed with love for us, he came down from heaven to redeem us. For our sake he endured every torment of body and soul and shrank from no bodily pain. He himself gave us an example of perfect patience and love. We, then, are to be patient in adversity."

— St. Francis of Paola

2/13/18

VERSE OF THE DAY

"How blessed is the man who does not walk in the counsel of the wicked, nor stand in the path of sinners, nor sit in the seat of scoffers! But his delight is in the law of the Lord, and in His law he meditates day and night. He will be like a tree firmly planted by streams of water, which yields its fruit in its season, and its leaf does not wither; and in whatever he does, he prospers."

— Psalm 1: 1-3

2/14/18

This daily meditation is powerful and took my breath away. As I begin my Lenten journey...would I be ready to meet God face to face?

MEDITATION OF THE DAY

"Each of us must come to the evening of life. Each of us must enter on eternity. Each of us must come to that quiet, awful time, when we will appear before the Lord of the vineyard, and answer for the deeds done in the body, whether they be good or bad. That, my dear brethren, you will have to undergo...It will be the dread moment of expectation when your fate for eternity is in the balance, and when you are about to be sent forth as the companion of either saints or devils, without possibility of change. There can be no change; there can be no reversal. As that judgment decides it, so it will be for ever and ever. Such is the particular judgment...when we find ourselves by ourselves, one by one, in his presence, and have brought before us most vividly all the thoughts, words, and deeds of this past life. Who will be able to bear the sight of himself? And yet we shall be obliged steadily to confront ourselves and to see ourselves. In this life we shrink from knowing our real selves. We do not like to know how sinful we are. We love those who prophesy smooth things to us, and we are angry with those who tell us of our faults. But on that day, not one fault only, but all the secret, as well as evident, defects of our character will be clearly brought out. We shall see what we feared to see here, and much more. And then, when the full sight of ourselves comes to us, who will not wish that he had known more of himself here, rather than leaving it for the inevitable day to reveal it all to him!"

— Blessed John Henry Newman,
p.101, *A Year with the Saints*

2/14/18

Time in Tucson is precious. Any of you who know me have probably heard me say how much I love the smell of Tucson after it rains! The creosote in the desert has a unique and beautiful smell. Of all the places we have lived, none have the aromas like Tucson in rain. I wish I could bottle it. It truly is part of my healing. God must know I need every full experience of my roots.

The rain was completely unexpected because it doesn't usually rain that much in the winter here. It is blessing my sadness and helping me to breathe in the holiness of home.

Today I spoke with the victims advocate from the D.A.'s office. My heart truly knows our son would have been the peacemaker, and Frank Loret de Mola would continue to live love, forgiveness, and hope. I have some ideas that should keep me very busy once I get home. I believe our sons and Henry want to be a part of getting Highway 120 fixed so no other family has to lose their family member or friend on the stretch of road known as "Blood Alley." Four people died in 2017 on the same road that took Franko. NO MORE! It was a horrible accident, and I bet all the other deaths on that road from previous years were also that...horrible accidents.

Please pray for our family to find the right people and the correct direction needed to fix Highway 120.

Thanks!

More 2/14/18

As I begin my Lenten Journey, I have decided to not give up anything, but to give. I will pray more and listen more to God's will in my life. I won't fear tomorrow. I will just live it as if it were my last.

This Lent has a whole new meaning for me. I am walking the Via do lo Rosa and taking each step methodically and deliberately toward my spiritual growth. Frank Loret de Mola's death will not crush me. It will create in me a new heart of understanding, forgiveness, and love!

Silence will come and go through these next forty days. But I will welcome the silence as I find my way closer to a God Who loves me more than infinity allows.

Find your holy place within, with me, on this unknown journey and breathe it in. Exhale out the negativity that might eat at your soul and find root in a place in your brain space. Move it out. No one even knows how bugged you might be with someone's behavior or lack of behavior. Remove that thought…Breathe and breathe again. I have to take my own advice.

I welcome the Holy Spirit to move into the brain space when I remove the negative spots, and The Spirit is welcome to move in, put their feet up, and take over the navigation system of my soul.

Blessed be God, oh blessed be God,

Who calls us by name,

Who calls us by name.

Holy and Chosen One!

Holy and Chosen One.

No more time for wrestling with the "what ifs." Time to dig deeper than I ever have and reach a new place of love. And at the end of this journey, I know I will find love, and God is love, and love is God.

2/15/18

VERSE OF THE DAY

"Blessed be the God and Father of our Lord Jesus Christ! By his great mercy he has given us a new birth into a living hope through the resurrection of Jesus Christ from the dead, and into an inheritance that is imperishable, undefiled, and unfading, kept in heaven for you, who are being protected by the power of God through faith for salvation ready to be revealed in the last time."

— 1 Peter 1:3-5

2/16/18

Lent:

> This desert is not a
> waste-land...
> For me:
> This desert is a
> FILL-LAND

"You must accept your cross; if you bear it courageously it will carry you to Heaven."

— St. John Vianney

2/17/18

"Great love can change small things into great ones, and it is only love which lends value to our actions."

— St. Faustina Kowalska

VERSE OF THE DAY

"I hold back my feet from every evil way, in order to keep your word. I do not turn away from your ordinances, for you have taught me. How sweet are your words to my taste, sweeter than honey to my mouth! Through your precepts I get understanding; therefore, I hate every false way."

— Psalm 119:101-4

2/18/18

And I end the day in love...being thankful for days behind me...thankful for days ahead...missing this beautiful son of ours...knowing he is still with us always. I love you, Franko. You would have loved seeing all these pictures.

Even if you weren't in Arizona much after your teen years, you loved the family and they love you.

2/19/18

We shall steer safely through every storm, so long as our heart is right, our intention fervent, our courage steadfast, and our trust fixed on God."

— St. Francis de Sales

2/20/18

"Start by doing what is necessary; then do what is possible; and suddenly you are doing the impossible."

— St. Francis of Assisi

When in the courtroom, I asked St. Michael the Archangel to protect us. There was so much going on in the courtroom...prisoners and their crimes, cries from families, and confusion. I didn't want to feel all the pain...but I did. St. Michael, protect us from words we hear that hurt. Protect us from those who want to cause pain. St. Michael, pray for us. I ask for prayers for Michael Sanchez, who drove the car in Frank Loret de Mola's death. I forgive you, Michael. It was a horrible accident. Now do something to help fix Highway 120.

2/21/18

When I was in Jerusalem, I asked God for a sign. He clearly answered me through a person on the pilgrimage...but it took me time to realize it. Then God gave me people, Mary Dresel and Deacon Dan, to help me see the sign was answered...clearly.

Throughout my life I have asked God for signs. When I seek signs, I don't find them. It is when I least expect answers to prayer that the results are there...in front of my face...if I just open my eyes and ears...

Gus Lloyd began my contemplation today and was what caused me to praise God this morning.

"The Signs are Everywhere"

"The first reading today is from Jonah 3. Jonah goes into the city of Nineveh and calls them to repent. (Jonah comes up again in the Mass.)

"In the Gospel reading from Luke 11, Jesus says to the crowd, 'This generation is an evil generation; it seeks a sign, but no sign will be given it except the sign of Jonah.' What was the sign of Jonah? One coming to preach repentance. Unfortunately, it is a sign that most choose to ignore. Jesus ends with, 'There is something greater than Jonah here.' Jesus is more than just a prophet, more than just a preacher. He is the Son of God. Here's your sign...

"Have you ever asked God for a sign? I think we all have at some time. When we're just not sure if God is there; when we don't know which way to turn. 'God, give me a sign!' I don't think there is anything wrong with asking God for a sign. The problem comes in when we ask God for something specific of our own making. Let me give you an example: 'God, if you turn this glass of water into wine, then I'll do what you ask of me. That will be my sign.' (By the way, that one's already been done.) I believe God gives us signs all the time. The signs are everywhere. The question is, are we being attentive? Are we open to the many ways God communicates with us? Ask the Holy Spirit today to open your eyes to see the signs all around you.

"Father, open our eyes, our hearts, our minds that we may see the many signs and signals you give us today to lead us along the right path. Amen."

2/21/18
Elizabeth Betty Loebe Poffinbarger, Trish Smith, Laura Loebe...didn't we JUST talk about this?

Oh...WOW! Sometimes written words are LOUD AND CLEAR as they appear on paper. Today's reflection is GORGEOUS and MUCH needed!

February 21, 2018
"Put aside your hatred and animosity. Take pains to refrain from sharp words. If they escape your lips, do not be ashamed to let your lips produce the remedy, since they have caused the wounds. Pardon one another so that later on you will not remember the injury. The recollection of an injury is itself wrong. It adds to our anger, nurtures our sin and hates what is good. It is a rusty arrow and poison for the soul. It puts all virtue to flight."

— St. Francis of Paola

Arraignment tomorrow. Please pray for Michael Sanchez. Pray for the judge. Pray for all involved in Frank Loret de Mola's case. Especially pray for Enrique Loret de Mola, my husband, Frank's dad. Pray for all who attend. Pray for families and friends who find it hard to forgive... Pray for our children and loved ones to be safe, especially while driving.

I thank everyone who has prayed for our family throughout this time. Thank you so much. The days have been better, and I know being in the desert has truly helped. I cry...But I am also finding laughter. I praise God for the momentum I am finding in my journey...momentum of love. Heal me from within, Lord, as I continue to come to You. Father, this long road can be steep and rocky, but You are my light, and I will sing songs of thanksgiving for each day I breathe. I praise You, God, for Frank's life that continues through Polly, Gina, and others we don't know. He will never be gone... Always and forever in my heart.

2/22/18

Just heard from Enrique Loret de Mola...Met and hugged Michael (the young man who accidentally killed Frank) and his Dad...tears...Another arraignment in March. I don't understand that...But THANK YOU for all your prayers! THIS is prayer answered. My heart is filled with thanksgiving because of connections made, and blessings are beginning.

2/23/18

February 23, 2018
"I will attempt day by day to break my will into pieces. I want to do God's Holy Will, not my own."

— St. Gabriel

2/24/18

In the quiet of the early morning, I find peace. I find tears. I find my soul longing to understand Christ and to connect with His love because I know I can't live this aching alone. I always have my family and friends to strengthen me. But in those moments when no one on earth hears me crying...God does, and that's when I call out from the depths of my soul...help me! Help me! Help me! Help me...

And I begin to breathe again. I begin to accept the reality, but I don't have to like it. And I beg God to give me back moments, and time, and people who have gone...and Frank Loret de Mola...And in my quiet, I see his beautiful face and kiss him again. And again. I say I love you, my Son. I say I miss you, my Son. And each moment I do that, my heart breaks a little more. And it is okay. I can take it because I was blessed to be the mother of four incredible people who live in me forever. I am blessed to forever be their mother. And a gentle smile comes as my thankfulness turns to Christ who gave to Henry and I gifts of true love... through our sons.

So, my tears subside again for a little while until the next moment when God fills me with hope, understanding, and peace, and comforts me as a grieving mother needs and deserves to be comforted. I walk this path, not knowing where I'm going...but open to where I will end because I have faith that all of this is for a purpose far greater than I can understand.

His girlfriend shared this gorgeous picture...tears flowed...memories sung in my mind...and love is obviously visible through the eyes of our Son, Frank Loret de Mola. Can't help but say...what if? I am positive he knows how much I miss him!

2/25/18

Yes...I understand this and will always!

> "Who except God can give you peace? Has the world ever been able to satisfy the heart?"
>
> — St. Gerard Majella

2/26/18

> "O Sacred Heart of Jesus, fountain of eternal life, Your Heart is a glowing furnace of Love. You are my refuge and my sanctuary."
>
> — St. Gertrude the Great

Yes! Amen!

We have heard this scripture in its entirety at many weddings.

VERSE OF THE DAY

"For now we see in a mirror dimly, but then face to face; now I know in part, but then I will know fully just as I also have been fully known. But now faith, hope, love, abide these three; but the greatest of these is love."

1 Corinthians 13:12-13

Frank Loret de Mola

Some days the memories knock the wind out of me.

2/27/18

"Love is the most beautiful sentiment the Lord has put into the soul of men and women."

— St. Gianna Molla

VERSE OF THE DAY

"O God, you are my God, I seek you, my soul thirsts for you; my flesh faints for you, as in a dry and weary land where there is no water. So I have looked upon you in the sanctuary, beholding your power and glory. Because your steadfast love is better than life, my lips will praise you. So I will bless you as long as I live; I will lift up my hands and call on your name."

Psalm 63:1-4

More...

This brought tears. So true...especially now...I miss you, Frank Loret de Mola. Every minute of the day I miss you. I miss Enrique Loret de Mola, Nick Loret de Mola, Alex Loret de Mola, and David Loret de Mola. I will be home on the twenty-fourth...maybe sooner...getting homesick for you all! Jacob and Emma, Nana will be home soon! I love you!

2/27/18 more

Since Frank Loret de Mola's death on September 22, so many friends have passed on. So many people I know have lost their spouses, their children, their brothers, or sisters. I honestly thought my heart couldn't take any more...but I can. I hold close friends as if you are my family. Since being in Tucson, two friends are going through the hardest time of loss. We all ask, "Why?" I am so sorry for what I continue to experience because now they are going through the pain. I love you. You know who you are. My prayers for peace are deep and continuous! God be with all of us!

I miss you, my Son!

2/28/18

Two years ago...Life has really changed now, but I am hopeful for all of us for our futures. I love my family!

From 2/28/2016

Well...Alex Loret de Mola is off...Oh God, how I already miss him. You know, life just is unpredictable...I always dreamed our sons would be next door to us. But life took other directions...Where will Enrique Loret de Mola and I be in five years? Where will our sons be? Our grandkids? Our family? Our journey continues as we head back to Phoenix to fly home. Thank you, especially, to Alex for flying out to spend time with family; to GG, Laura Loebe for making our stay so wonderful; as always, to Patrick; Trish Smith, for flying out, I loved spending time with you and eating popsicles with you. For Phil and Anna, Elizabeth Betty Loebe Poffinbarger, Daniel Poffinbarger, Paul Loebe, Irma, Kathie Loebe, Steve Ware, Christina Soto, Joshua Loebe, Mok Loebe; Elina Loebe for your love and FUN, shots, and photos, pinata, food, LAUGHTER and more love, thank you! It was an incredible time! It was wonderful to begin the fun with our Loebe side of the family andAunt

Penny Lowe, Uncle Dan, Aunt Pam, Uncle Ken, Candy Vogel, and John Vogel, and I only wish I could have seen my Loebe cousins. Crazy week, my cousins! I promise we WILL get together! All my Vasquez, Morales, and Martinez family, I love you beyond words! You mean the world to me! We grew up in a world where cousins were more like siblings. You are a part of my heart—a HUGE part! Thank you for all the hard work! Next time can we have a day's break in between each reunion so us old folks can recuperate? Lololol. Love you all. My heart is joyful and emotional all at the same time! Mike Morales, Anne Morales, Amy Morales Baum, and Austin Baum, Henry and I want to thank you for the gifts you blessed us with by hosting all of us! It was AMAZING!

God bless our family as new life begins with three more births coming soon. God bless our family as we age gracefully...Please God! God bless our family, and let us NEVER forget where we came from...Abe, Abuelito, the incredible Papa and our beautiful Mama! I thank God daily for all! Praise the Lord, my soul!

3/2/18

"Act as if everything depended on you; trust as if everything depended on God."

— St. Ignatius of Loyola

Woke up early...quiet...I can hear silence. I welcome silence. I listen for the ponderings in my heart. They come. Franko, Kurt, Jackie, JoJo, Paul, Terri, Angelo's wife, friends of friend's family, Dad, Gayle, and so many others come to my mind as I lay here praying and thinking about heaven. I am not awake just to be awake. I know there's meaning in this not sleeping stuff... I see meaning...I find this time of the morning to be an opportunity to spiritually grow. Sometimes it is time to just be. Other times it is time to say a rosary...which I don't do often enough. So here I am... All of me....

3/3/18

And again…3:30 A.M. is my time to settle my thoughts, think of God, the Father, His Son, and the Holy Spirit. I hold Mary, our incredible Mother and example of selfless love, so close to my heart. And I talk with Franko. How can I not cry? It just happens when I think of the things I wish I would have done for him and with him. I realized this morning that I used to think people should never regret anything when a loved one dies. I have a few regrets. I regret I didn't see him enough. I regret I didn't hug him enough. I regret I didn't get enough pictures of him or pictures with him. Stupid, probably. But real. I never regretted anything when my dad died because I moved to Tucson to help my mom. Never any big regrets. The "what ifs" with Frankie are probably normal. But painful. Sometimes waking up at 3:30 A.M. just stinks! But I need it. Healing in the desert continues….

> "Prayer purifies us, reading instructs us. Both are good when both are possible. Otherwise, prayer is better than reading."
>
> — St. Isidore of Seville

3/4/18

I believe because I can. I believe because I want to. I believe because I have seen miracles. I believe because I believe. No explanations needed…I just do! Amen!

3/6/18

Forgiveness has never been as clear in my life as it is now! Please read Gus Lloyd's reflection for today…It truly has blessed me. Thank you, Gus!

> "What Eating an Elephant and Forgiveness Have in Common"
>
> "Today's first reading from Daniel 3 contains one of the most beautiful and heartfelt prayers in all of Scripture. It is the prayer

of Azariah, while he was in the fiery furnace. Take some time today to read it over; to pray the prayer with Azariah. I think you'll be touched.

"In the Gospel reading from Matthew 18, Peter asked Jesus, 'How often must I forgive? As many as seven times?' Jesus replies, 'Not seven times, but seventy-seven times.' Some translations render it 'seventy times seven times.' Of course, Jesus means that there should be no end to our forgiveness, just as there is no end to God's forgiveness. But what's in a number? I want to offer a different perspective today. I would say that we need to forgive once. Controversial? Let me explain.

"Have you ever heard this question: How do you eat an elephant? The answer is one bite at a time. Don't think about the whole elephant. Just take that first bite, and think only about that. I believe the same principle applies with forgiveness. If we think about having to forgive someone who has hurt us or offended us over and over again, 490 times even, it can easily overwhelm us. God, I just can't do that! It's an elephant! And God says, okay, fine. Can you take just one bite—forgive just this one time? And that's all we need. If anger and resentment and bitterness rear their ugly heads again somewhere down the road, even a few seconds later, then all we have to do is take another bite - forgive right then. Just once. Try it today. Take that first bite of the elephant. Forgive, just once.

"Father, give us the grace to forgive, just once, just for now. We thank you in Jesus' name. Amen."

"Our true worth does not consist in what human beings think of us. What we really are consists in what God knows us to be."

— St. John Berchmans

This is sooo perfect for me for today! I woke up with this paraphrased quote from Psalm 19:14: "Let the words of my mouth, be pleasing to You, Pleasing to You." Fernando Ortega has a gorgeous version of this song: "Let the Words of My Mouth." Please listen, if so led!

3/7/18

I woke up at 3:00 A.M. today...again! But this time I was thinking about how I should share and "teach" more about faith. I thought about the boys when they were little and how I should have talked more to them about faith and beliefs. I also thought about the fact that I didn't ever think about teaching faith; I just tried to live it but fell short. A LOT!

The beliefs I have now are so much clearer to me that "teaching" it makes more sense because I understand so much more. It should be easier to share my journey. Then I read Gus Lloyd's reflection and...POW BOOM ZOW... I thought he read my mind...NO! The God I love is alive so clearly in today's readings. Even if I can't or don't make it to Mass...I can read His word daily, and Gus helps me understand and meditate on God's life lessons. These lessons are for ALL!

Here is Gus Lloyd's reflection. Thank you, Gus for speaking to my heart through your faith! Amen!

"Teaching the Faith"

"There's a word that comes up in both of the readings today. That word is teach. In the first reading from Deuteronomy 4, Moses tells the people, 'However, take care and be earnestly on your guard not to forget the things which your own eyes have seen, nor let them slip from your memory as long as you live, but teach them to your children and to your children's children's children.' "In the Gospel reading from Matthew 5, Jesus says, 'But whoever obeys and teaches these commandments will be called the greatest in the Kingdom of heaven.'

As parents, we are the first teachers of our children. We cannot leave teaching the faith to someone else. But this goes way beyond just family. We must be teachers of the faith to everyone. It starts with example—living the faith. But we must also know how to explain the faith to those who question us. Perhaps this is why so many are reticent to talk about their faith—because they don't know it themselves. Now that we're in the second half of Lent, spend some time learning the faith, that you may teach it to others and help them understand.

Father, give us an ever-greater hunger to learn our faith. Give us the boldness to teach it to others. Amen."

3/8/18

Gus Lloyd's words hit my soul today.

I can go along each day smoothly...thinking "I've got this thing called life!" Then suddenly... without any clue...the proverbial rug not only gets pulled out from under me...but it leaves me no floor below, and I fall to a place I never ever wanted to go. Darkness is not a place I have known for a very long time in my life. And I NEVER want to stay there.

Gus speaks of armoring ourselves, because I KNOW the closer I get to God my Father, the more the attacks come from the dark side to get me off course and keep me from truth. I have experienced this in my life...as I will always because I am a believer in HIM. I have to keep my armor up and be aware of my failings. I am a human who just wants to love.

"Fully Armed"

"Today's first reading from Jeremiah 7 should be required reading. See if you don't recognize that exactly what was happening then is happening now. 'Say to them: This is the nation that does not listen to the voice of the Lord, its God, or take correction. Faithfulness has disappeared; the word itself is banished from their speech.'

"In the Gospel reading from Luke 11, Jesus is accused of driving out demons by the power of Beelzebul. He then talks about how a kingdom divided against itself cannot stand. His remarks include this: 'When a strong man fully armed guards his palace, his possessions are safe.'

Are you fully armed? Of course, I'm not talking about guns and knives and earthly weapons here. I'm talking about spiritual weapons. Prayer, fasting, almsgiving. Scripture, the Rosary and Holy Mass. Read about the armor of God in Ephesians 6. If you are not fully armed with these spiritual weapons, then you're easy prey for Satan. Arm yourself for battle today!!

Father, may we make use of all the spiritual weapons at our disposal. Help us to be bold, courageous, and fully armed for battle. Amen."

"Happiness can only be achieved by looking inward and learning to enjoy whatever life has, and this requires transforming greed into gratitude."

— St. John Chrysostom

3/9/18

How do I love my neighbor? Even...DO I love my neighbor?

Neighbor is the homeless person. Neighbor is the person who doesn't agree with my beliefs. Neighbor is the person so difficult to love or even like. Neighbor is you. Neighbor is me.

Gus Lloyd's Reflection:

"Got It?"

"What a beautiful first reading we have today from Hosea 14. God tells the people, 'Say to him, 'We shall say no more, 'Our god,' to the work of our hands.' 'I will heal their defection,' says the Lord, 'I will love them freely.' In the Gospel passage from

Mark 12, Jesus is asked which is the first of all the command-ments. He answers with two: You shall love the Lord, your God and love your neighbor as yourself.

"A scribe replies affirming Jesus, saying that the two com-mandments are 'worth more than all burnt offerings and sacrifices.' When Jesus saw that he answered with understanding, he said to him, 'You are not far from the Kingdom of God.' Wow! Quite the compliment, no? How I would love to hear Jesus say those words to me. And the reason He said this is because the scribe "got it.

"There are times in my life when I really get it. The true mes-sage of love for God and love of neighbor goes right to the core of my soul. Unfortunately, there are also times when I don't get it. I let my own pride, anger, or selfishness get in the way of getting it. It's a good thing that God is very patient with me. When it comes to understanding God's ways, I really, really want to get it!

Father, help us to get it today. Help us to understand more and more how to love You more and love our neighbor more. Amen."

3/9/18

"Realize it, my brethren; everyone who breathes, high and low, educated and ignorant, young and old, man and woman, has a mission, has a work. We are not sent into this world for nothing; we are not born at random; God sees every one of us; He creates every soul, He lodges it in the body, one by one, for a purpose. He needs, He deigns to need, every one of us. He has an end for each of us; we are all equal in His sight, and we are placed in our different ranks and stations, not to get what we can out of them for ourselves, but to labor in them for Him. As Christ has His work, we too have ours; as He rejoiced to do His work, we must rejoice in ours also."

— Blessed John Henry Newman

3/10/18

Healing comes in all forms...music, laughter, crying, and quiet. Tonight was laughter... the kind of laughter that feels as good as a deep and sobbing cry. Yes...

3/11/18

I believe this now more than ever...It's called...

FRANKtitude! Thank you, my Son, Frank Loret de Mola, for teaching me this!

Megan Bliss: In order to truly live, you must forgive.

> March 11, 2018
>
> "When an evil thought is presented to the mind, we must immediately endeavor to turn our thoughts to God, or to something which is indifferent. But the first rule is, instantly to invoke the names of Jesus and Mary and to continue to invoke them until the temptation ceases. He who trusts in himself is lost. He who trusts in God can do all things."
>
> — St. Alphonsus Liguori

3/12/18

Prayer for each other is powerful! See Gus Lloyd's reflection and know that when we pray for each other, possible healing can occur...

Gus Lloyd:

"Intercessory Prayer"

"Ever wonder what things will be like after Jesus returns? That is, after all, a basic tenet of our faith; that Christ will come again.

Well, wonder no more! The prophet Isaiah gives us a beautiful picture of 'the new heavens and the new earth.' Check it out. 'There shall always be rejoicing and happiness...No longer shall the sound of weeping be heard there, or the sound of crying.' Nice, huh.

"Our Gospel reading today is from John 4. This part of John's Gospel is called The Book of Signs. And today we read about the second sign Jesus did when he came to Galilee from Judea. A man comes and asks Jesus to go to his home and heal his son, who is dying. Jesus says to him, 'Unless you people see signs and wonders, you will not believe.' Undaunted by the rebuke, the man persists. Jesus says to him, 'You may go; your son will live.' And from that moment on, the boy was healed.

"This is another wonderful example of how Jesus used the faith of another to perform a miracle healing. If you have ever been doubtful about intercessory prayer, doubt no more. This father interceded on behalf of his son. Jesus did not need to physically lay hands on the boy. The faith of his father was enough. So, who will you intercede for today? Who can you bring to Jesus today in faith?

"Father, hear our prayers as we offer up our children, spouses, friends and family to Jesus in faith. Touch them and heal them in your great mercy. Amen."

More 3/12/18

This is so relevant in our lives now...

"Force yourself, if necessary, always to forgive those who offend you, from the very first moment. For the greatest injury or offense you can suffer from them, is nothing compared to what God has forgiven you."

— St. Josemaria Escriva

I cried.

Haven't done that much in a while.

My friends comforted me.

I am so thankful for Carlota Agard and Nancy Tran being in Tucson.

Mom is sleeping.

The wave of pain engulfed me.

Surprised me.

Unexpected.

My heart misses yours, Frank Loret de Mola...

My heart misses you.

3/14/18

VERSE OF THE DAY

"Devote yourselves to prayer, keeping alert in it with thanksgiving. Conduct yourselves wisely toward outsiders, making the most of the time. Let your speech always be gracious, seasoned with salt, so that you may know how you ought to answer everyone."

— Colossians 4:2-6

3/15/18

Who or what is YOUR light? I know mine.

Without my light, I would have never walked ahead to the next minute of each day.

There have been times, in the past almost six months, that I felt despair, but never hopelessness. I have felt grief beyond any understanding, but my head has been above water. I have lived life in complete disbelief of what happened on September 22, 2017 but extremely aware that I will meet our Son again in God's time.

Still trying to find what new normal is or what it will be like. Sometimes it is a very lonely thought. Sometimes I still don't believe it all happened, even though I was there...in the hospital room...seeing Frank being forced air to save his body he so generously gave so that others can live.

Still hard to believe, but I am just going to accept, pray, and patiently wait for another day to begin to start the process over again.

Missing my Franko. A lot! Waves of love pouring over me as God leads me on!

3/16/18
Lent continues...

When I swear, am I imitating Christ?

When I speak badly about someone, am I imitating Christ?

When I don't treat others with respect, am I imitating Christ?

Gus Lloyd's reflection today gave me questions to ponder...and work on!

"Different Ways"

"The first reading today is an Old Testament prophecy of the Messiah from the Book of Wisdom. Read it and see how it was fulfilled perfectly in the person of Jesus. In the Gospel reading from John 7, Jesus begins to reveal more about Himself, and how He was sent by the Father.

'To us he is the censure of our thought; merely to see him is a hardship. Because his life is not like that of others, and different are his ways.'

"We know that Jesus' life was not like that of others. His ways were different. As Christians, we are called to imitate Christ. So this begs the question: are our ways different? Or are we acting just like non-believers that surround us? Would anyone notice that we act differently than the world? Or have we become so entrenched in the ways of the world that there is no difference in the way we act? Something to ponder today...

"Father, help us to order our lives as Jesus did—to be different than the world. May we imitate Him in all we say and do. Amen."

More 3/16/18

Frank Loret de Mola...his face...my heart stopped...Yes...Frank Loret de Mola, Nick Loret de Mola, Alex Loret de Mola, David Loret de Mola, Enrique Loret de Mola, and many others share this name...My heart is bound with all...

Tucson friends, I have not seen many of you. It is not on purpose. I have been busy with going back and forth with my siblings. I have had my best friend from Sahuaro High over for one night to catch up. Two friends came to visit from Sacramento to spend time with Mom and I. I have had a couple of days of meltdowns and time for reflection. I have spent time with a friend whose youngest brother died, and I am honored to sing at his funeral the day I leave. I have spent time with Mom, Laura Loebe, and Auntie Yolanda Martinez. I will spend time with cousins next week...but never enough time! I am missing time with many cousins, and I am so sorry! I leave on the twenty-fourth, and I can't believe I have been here already a month. Each day has been full, and I am thankful for all this time. My husband is amazing and supportive of his crazy wife...He knows me so well. He knows my love of this desert and my deep need for home.

I have two homes: Tucson and Sacramento. Both are loved. Too bad they are separated by eight-hundred-plus miles!

Please forgive me for the lack of time. I go with the flow...God's flow... Another time...

3/17/18

I woke up thinking of Franko...then saw Gus Lloyd's reflection. I never knew this prayer. It is attributed to St. Patrick...It is beautiful...deep and beautiful.

Gus Lloyd:

"St. Patrick's Breastplate"

"Happy St. Patrick's Day! I'm going to go a bit out of the normal today and not do a reflection on the daily readings. In honor of St. Patrick, I want to share with you the beautiful St. Patrick's Breastplate. Many people may know a small part of this beautiful prayer (specifically the next-to-last stanza), but few have ever read it all. I think it deserves our attention. So pray and enjoy!"

'I bind unto myself today
The strong name of the Trinity,
By invocation of the same,
The Three in One and One in Three.
I bind this day to me for ever,
By the power of faith, Christ's Incarnation;
His baptism in the Jordan River;
His death on a cross for my salvation;
His bursting from the spicèd tomb;
His riding up the heavenly way;
His coming at the day of doom;
I bind unto myself today.
I bind unto myself the power
Of the great love of the Cherubim;
The sweet 'Well done' in judgment hour;
The service of the Seraphim,
Confessors' faith, Apostles' word,
The Patriarchs' prayers, the Prophets' scrolls,

All good deeds done unto the Lord,
And purity of virgin souls.
I bind unto myself today
The virtues of the starlit heaven,
The glorious sun's life-giving ray,
The whiteness of the moon at even,
The flashing of the lightning free,
The whirling wind's tempestuous shocks,
The stable earth, the deep salt sea,
Around the old eternal rocks.
I bind unto myself today
The power of God to hold and lead,
His eye to watch, His might to stay,
His ear to hearken to my need.
The wisdom of my God to teach,
His hand to guide, his shield to ward,
The word of God to give me speech,
His heavenly host to be my guard.
Against the demon snares of sin,
The vice that gives temptation force,
The natural lusts that war within,
The hostile men that mar my course;
Or few or many, far or nigh,
In every place and in all hours
Against their fierce hostility,
I bind to me these holy powers.
Against all Satan's spells and wiles,
Against false words of heresy,
Against the knowledge that defiles,
Against the heart's idolatry,
Against the wizard's evil craft,
Against the death-wound and the burning
The choking wave and the poisoned shaft,
Protect me, Christ, till thy returning.

Christ be with me, Christ within me,
Christ behind me, Christ before me,
Christ beside me, Christ to win me,
Christ to comfort and restore me,
Christ beneath me, Christ above me,
Christ in quiet, Christ in danger,
Christ in the hearts of all that love me,
Christ in mouth of friend and stranger.
I bind unto myself the name,
The strong name of the Trinity;
By invocation of the same.
The Three in One, and One in Three,
Of whom all nature hath creation,
Eternal Father, Spirit, Word:
Praise to the Lord of my salvation,
salvation is of Christ the Lord.'

"It is a lesson we all need—to let alone the things that do not concern us. He has other ways for others to follow Him; all do not go by the same path. It is for each of us to learn the path by which He requires us to follow Him, and to follow Him in that path."

— St. Katharine

More 3/17/18

God's plan isn't always expected. I know when He places things in front of me for a reason. I am singing to thank God for Kurt's life. I am honored beyond words. Pray for my Kanzler family friends. Amen!

3/18/18

It is 3:20 A.M. I am reading email, and Gus Lloyd's reflection is there. I completely understand what he is talking about. However, am I really living it? Am I giving up the things that keep me from growing spiritually because of selfishness? Or am I finding every excuse to continue keeping God at arm's length so I don't have to change?

Lent leads me to a deeper sense of what needs to change in me. But it is hard. It is never easy to take the next steps needed to give God the space He so rightly deserves in my life. He never gives up on me. But do I give up on Him?

Gus Lloyd's reflection:

"Dying to Produce Fruit"

"In our Gospel reading today from John 12, Jesus teaches us about wheat. 'Amen, amen, I say to you, unless a grain of wheat falls to the ground and dies, it remains just a grain of wheat; but if it dies, it produces much fruit.' So, what does a grain of wheat falling to the ground and dying have to do with us?

Dying to produce fruit? At face value, it makes no sense. I mean, don't we have to live and grow and flourish to produce fruit? Well, yes. But like a grain of wheat, there is a process that we must go through. And, as Christians, the first part of the process is dying. No, not physical death. That will be the beginning of another process. Jesus is talking about dying to self. About 'killing off' our own selfish passions and desires and living for Christ, living for others.

Death is a very difficult thing. It is hard for us to let go of those we love. It can be equally as hard, if not harder, to let go of our selfishness. But let go we must. By ourselves, this is impossible. But as Jesus teaches us, with God all things are possible. Even willfully dying.

Father, we want to produce fruit for the Kingdom. Help us

to die to ourselves, that we might serve you by serving our brothers and sisters here. Amen."

3/21/18

Leaving Tucson this Saturday. I have been in PineTop with my generous cousin, Yolie Cox; my Auntie Yolanda Martinez, cousin Laura Hall, Martha Martinez, and my beautiful mom, Laura Loebe. It has been a great way to end my stay in Arizona. I also am very aware that I have taken time to heal from such an unfathomable loss and heartbreak.

At times I feel as if time has sped up and made the pain seem in the distant past. Other moments I catch my breath as I feel as if I saw Frankie yesterday...or was it the day before? I almost can't breathe until I remember it has been six months already. I can't even believe it's already been six months...I just want to see your face again and smile because you laughed about something Jacob did or said.

A mother's sadness never ends, it seems. A part of my life is missing. There is no doubt. There is no turning back. There IS hope for believers. Oh if only everyone could have hope. I believe Frank can hear me when I call his name or ask him to pray for us. I believe he misses us as much as we miss him. I believe his work has begun in a new realm and depth that I can't even imagine. I believe he knows he will see us again and will welcome us. Because if I don't believe in the hereafter...what is there?

My solid ground is my faith. My firm foundation has helped me through the long nights. You see, it is when I go to bed that I take pause to cry. I find time to miss people I have loved who are gone. I also miss Henry, Nicolas, Alex, and David because I find my home in them. They are the ones who helped make me the person I am today...by God's grace.

And another night begins...prayer time...reminiscing time...time to shut off all other thoughts and focus on love. I feel thankful and blessed.

Amen!

3/22/18
FRANKtitude...

3/23/18

I have truly learned all of my life how important forgiveness, forgiving, and being forgiven can be and how it impacts my life. Nowhere has this rung truer than now, as I understand the depth and meaning of the death of our son, Frank Loret de Mola.

From the moment I heard that Frank was in an accident not caused by him, I already began to forgive Michael. I didn't even know his name or if he was male or female...I just began to forgive. Frank would have wanted that. He knew very well how to forgive. He forgave me for the mistakes I made as his mom. And he still loved me. That is called UNCONDITIONAL love. Henry and I raised our sons to live unconditional love. How many times did I love them through some very difficult times...no matter what? Always and forever!

This Lent has been a time of healing in the Tucson desert. This is where I learned how to live and forgive. If there is anything I can share that this old lady has learned...forgive. If we keep anger or vengeance toward people, we are giving them way too much space in our brains, hearts, and souls. Forgiveness is free. Forgiveness is real. Forgiveness is healing for you, Me, and those who have hurt us.

I choose to live my life forgiving!

I choose to live my life expecting to love and forgive.

I choose to live my life in prayerful hope of being forgiven. If that doesn't happen, I will continue to love...UNCONDITIONALLY...always...

3/23/18

"Keep the joy of loving God in your heart and share this joy with all you meet, especially your family. Be holy."

— St. Mother Teresa of Calcutta

3/26/18

This meditation is perfect for today as we travel to another arraignment. God bless this process and let all involved follow Your will as I place my trust in You.

"O man, when the world hates you and is faithless toward you, think of your God, how he was struck and spat upon. You should not accuse your neighbor of guilt, but pray to God that he be merciful to you both."

— St. Nicholas of Flue

MEDITATION OF THE DAY
"This world is filled with many vulgar and dishonorable things that will claw and tear at your Christian purity if you allow them to. Don't let them! Seek instead the things of God. He will purify you and free you from your slavery to profane and inconsequential things."

— Patrick Madrid

3/26/18 more

Went to the arraignment again today. Again, it's been postponed...This is truly a long process...On April 25 we will try again!

Tears...Words of apology...More tears.

God be with us through this process. We need healing hearts. Nothing will bring Franko back, but if I allow forgiveness to set in completely, my healing will be great. I pray for all to have hearts of forgiveness and peace. Amen!

3/27/18

I need to really listen to this! Those who know and have a relationship with God can really understand this. Even in my toughest times...today happens to be emotionally tough...Why? Maybe from the arraignment being postponed again? Maybe really missing Franko. Maybe working on the ACTS Retreat prep and not knowing my place. Maybe because Emma is sick and she can't tell me what hurts. Maybe because I accidentally cut in front of a man going into the McDonald's and he told me off. Then I paid his $2.35 bill and he waved at me...Maybe there is no reason, and I just cry easily today...It's fine...In time I hope the tears aren't as often. I just came back from six weeks in the desert...and my heart belongs to both Sacramento and Tucson! Can everyone in Tucson just move to Sacramento until my grandkids get OLD? BUMMER! Pat Berg shared: "Those who leave everything in God's hands will eventually see God's hands in everything." Amen.

3/29/18

Woke up in tears but Jacob and Emma have blessed this day. She is feeling better, but I can tell she's not 100 percent yet. Love my grands!

> "Pray, hope and don't worry. Anxiety doesn't help at all. Our Merciful Lord will listen to your prayer."
>
> — Saint Padre Pio

May I say, we recently found out that all four recipients of Frank Loret de-Mola's life are healthy and doing great. I thank God for them and for Frank's gifts. Gina Pak Dela Cruz and Polly Bleavins are known to us. Maybe some-day we will know the other two. Until then, I thank and praise God for Polly and Gina and their incredible love of our son's gifts. Thank you both for all you have brought to our hearts. Love you ladies very much!

3/30/18

If I didn't believe this scripture, where would I be today? Last night I felt like I was beginning to fall apart again. At three thirty, I woke up and began to pray. I know Henry was right there…but when I pray, I am just me, God, Jesus, the Holy Spirit, and the Blessed Mother. I don't hear the house noises or the sounds of the town…just us. And I pray…sometimes nodding off in the middle of my talking to God. Sometimes reciting a Hail Mary to try and stay focused. I find great comfort. And I began asking Frank Loret de Mola…Franko, for his prayers. Anyone can. Sometimes I just say…"Hi, Son!"

More 3/30/18

When someone said something negative about my faith…this is what I said back:

> "I love the church. My closest friends are in the church. I love the rites and the depth of the meaning of the church. I would NEVER leave because I love that there are people coming to-gether who have similar positive thoughts about a home of peace. I don't go there because of the institution. I go there because it is what I LOVE. Not all of us agree politically…but we still come. Not all of us agree on all the doctrine, but we still come. Not all of us even understand our faith or take it as seriously, but we still come. It is not just a church journey in faith, it is a very personal journey with many avenues for growth, i.e. retreats, Bible studies,

leadership weekends, pilgrimages, holy hours, daily Mass, mission work, and so much more. This is truly not an INSTITUTION. It is a way of life. MY way. HIS WAY!

More 3/30/18

Good Friday...God's Friday...
the lintels splattered with blood now become the Christ.
He is crucified and by His blood, we are healed!
Wait, the resurrection is on its way!
Behold the Lamb of God!

3/30/18 again

On this day in 2016...Frank posted this:

"LJ and I will be taking over the studio, teaching them whippersnappers how it's done.
The Sacramento Kings of Shock Jock return to Kssu for their 25th anniversary.
The Beans and Rice show, one time only!
Getcha popcorn ready, 10:00 A.M. Tax Day!
Tune in at the KSSU Homepage, all day err day!"

Frank wrote back...

I said: "I'm getting my work computer ready to go!!!"
Frank said: "Haha! Not until April 15th mom. Don't run out of battery :)"
I said: "I saved the website, you are funny!!!!"

I miss you, my third baby. Oh so much!

More...same day

I think many of us in Sacramento are on emotion overload. Please be sure to breathe. Please be sure to sleep. Please be sure to drink lots of water. Please remember you are not alone. Please understand that empathy can suck you dry, and you don't realize it until you can't see up to look down. Please remember to take care of YOU! I am talking to myself too! Frank Loret de Mola's death has tested my ability to endure. It has given me tears I NEVER knew I had...hadn't cried in at least twenty-five years...no joke.

Franko's death has drained me, and I haven't been out there like so many of you. I realize I can't. I have to take my self-knowledge and hold tight to what I can and can't do. One day I think I can do ANYTHING...The next day I am drained from any energy I might have had.

Please take care. For those of you with faith, ask St. Michael the Archangel for protection with his prayers to God the Father.

Prayer for Protection to St. Michael:

"Saint Michael the Archangel,
defend us in battle.

Be our protection against the wickedness and snares of the devil.
May God rebuke him, we humbly pray;
and do Thou, O Prince of the Heavenly Host,
by the Divine Power of God,
cast into hell Satan and all the evil spirits
who roam throughout the world seeking the ruin of souls."

3/31/18

Today the Church takes a rest until tonight! Easter Vigil starts at 8:00 P.M. tonight, and it should be beautiful! Over seventy confirmande. Wow! I have a feeling I better bring a case of water! Four hours…here we come! Okay… maybe three!

God bless all receiving Confirmation and Baptism tonight all around the Catholic world! The Holy Spirit is ALIVE and well and living within all of us! Seek Him…He is real!

I call upon You, Holy Spirit, as we thank You for Your love and protection. So many Catholics have never received Confirmation, and now the church is seeing an awakening of hope. People wanting to be in full communion, and this is AMAZING!

4/1/18

"If you truly want to help the soul of your neighbor, you should approach God first with all your heart. Ask him simply to fill you with charity, the greatest of all virtues; with it you can accomplish what you desire."

— St. Vincent Ferrer

4/2/18

For those of us mourning the loss of someone we love, or dealing with financial loss, job loss, or any hardship...this!

2 Corinthians 4:17, New International Version (NIV):

"For our light and momentary troubles are achieving for us an eternal glory that far outweighs them all."

4/3/18

2 Corinthians 4:18, New International Version (NIV):

"So we fix our eyes not on what is seen, but on what is unseen, since what is seen is temporary, but what is unseen is eternal."

4/4/18

Yes...this is where I am...my heart...You taught me so much, Son...Keep teaching me! Pray for us, Franko! I love you!

VERSE OF THE DAY
"God, the Lord is my strength; he makes my feet like the feet of a deer, and makes me tread upon the heights."

— Habakkuk 3:19

4/5/18

Henry and I will take off for two nights and three days to a favorite place in San Simeon, sort of near the Hearst Castle. We are staying in a resort we have stayed in before and absolutely love. Our room is right on the beach... So, we can relax, listen to the waves hitting the shore, put the fireplace on in our room or soak in the jacuzzi...I don't care if it rains the entire time. I find healing, peace, Jesus, love, and prayer comes easily when I am in or near the ocean. I think Enrique Loret de Mola does too. Celebrating number forty-three on the eleventh of April... Thank You, God, for helping us get here! Blessed Mother, pray for us!

Cleaning day today. I haven't even FELT like cleaning much of anything for a VERY long time. Today I decided...it's time! So...beds are made, clean sheets, and a new mattress cover for our master bedroom, Jacob's room cleaned, bed made. Emma/Grammy's bedroom cleaned, bed is made. Kitchen, living and family room floors washed...A LOT! It's nice to walk on clean floors! I was going to take a walk but figured cleaning is just as good! Therapy!

4/7/18

"At each step we can admire the grandeur, the power, the goodness of God. How bountifully He provides for all our wants—I would even say for our pleasures!"

— St. Théodore Guérin

MEDITATION OF THE DAY

"Do not look for the faults of your friend. Do not repeat the shortcomings of your neighbors in your talk. You are not the judge of creation. You do not have dominion over the earth. If you love righteousness, admonish your soul and yourself. Be the judge of your own sins, and chastise your own transgressions."

— St. Ephrem the Syrian

4/8/18

My best friend from high school, Sahuaro High in Tucson, Arizona, is Nancy Cacioppo Bonner. This is an article about her youngest son, Tony, gunned down in Glendale, Arizona eleven years ago. She and her husband started a foundation that is helping so many! Tony was only twenty-three. He had served in the military, in Afghanistan…came home, became a police officer, and at a routine traffic stop was gunned down by a man who wanted to kill police. My friend and I will NEVER get over our sons' deaths. How can we? God bless Anthony "Tony" and our Frank Anthony Frank Loret de Mola! Hate being in this same club! HATE IT!

4/9/18

I honestly don't know where I would be if I didn't have a relationship with Jesus and his Mother, Mary. Gus Lloyd does a great job explaining Mary's place in my faith and possibly explains her role well enough for others to get a better idea of the high esteem given to her by the Catholic Church.

Thank you again, Gus!

"Our 'Yes'"

"Today we celebrate the Solemnity of the Annunciation of the Lord. Traditionally celebrated on March 25 (nine months before Christmas), when that date falls during Holy Week, the feast is moved to the first Monday after Easter Week. So, let me be the first to wish you a Merry Christmas this year! In the first reading, we see the prophecy from Isaiah: 'The virgin shall be with child, and bear a son, and shall name him Emmanuel, which means 'God is with us!"

The readings today all point toward Mary's fiat, which we see in Luke 1: 'Behold, I am the handmaid of the Lord. May it be done to me according to your word.' Perhaps our Responsorial Psalm for today, taken from Psalm 40, sums it up best. 'Here I am, Lord; I come to do your will.'

Mary has many titles in Catholic tradition. I think that one of my favorite ones, though not an official 'title,' is 'the first Christian.' Mary was the first one to truly accept Christ. She experienced a closeness with Christ that no one else ever would or could. Many non-Catholic Christian traditions have tried to diminish the role of Mary. Some see her as just an interchangeable cog in God's big wheel. Perhaps you've heard something like 'Mary was just a vessel.' Really? The womb that carried the Son of God, the breasts that nursed Him, the woman who loved every moment of His life, 'just a vessel?' Mary's role can never be diminished. Mary is the Ark of the New Covenant. She said yes at the Annunciation, and every other moment in her life. Do we?

Father, we thank you for the example of Mary, always saying yes to Your will. May we imitate her with our 'Yes' today and always. Amen."

4/9/18

"The Eucharist is the Sacrament of Love; It signifies Love. It produces love. The Eucharist is the consummation of the whole spiritual life."

— St. Thomas Aquinas

4/10/18

Before life changed…

Who was I?

I used to say…if I ever lost one of our sons, someone would have to lock me up! Believe me…there have been a few times I really thought I needed to be locked away…to just exist…to be left alone so I wouldn't have to be anyone anymore…

This brings me to today…not quite seven months since our lives took an unexpected path… winding…twisting…at times spewing and spinning out of control, in my mind. Oh, but my body knows the pain. Weight…UP. Tears…come out almost daily…not quite. Hair…loss. Tired…all the time. Exercise…bits at a time. Faith…stronger than ever.

You see me. I can laugh very hard at times, and oh that feels so good. What you don't see are my heart aches that catch my breath, mostly at two thirty in the morning. Tears come easy as I ask God permission to keep in communication with my son. And so, I whisper words of love so no one hears me. But I really want to scream my words.

Tears fall…and I beg for more time with him…lots more time…and I kind of feel like I get it…in my one-way conversation that I believe is heard.

Memories from a year ago…seems like ninety…

4/10/18 more

Today's thought…and hard to live by, but I'm trying…very hard! Trust in an unseen God is all about faith. I can feel Him working in my life, in fact, all of my life. He sent His Son, who was REALLY on this Earth…but I never saw Him. But, do you know what? I have met Him! Yes, I have. I have met Him in my family, friends, people who have helped me on my life's journey, strangers with a smile, strangers with sadness in their walk. I have seen Him when I don't want to see Him. He is there. He really is!

4/11/18

Today is number forty-three. To think...we were married in 1975. He was twenty-three, and I was nineteen. Our lives have taken us from Tucson to Butte, Montana. We lived in Butte for the first six months of our marriage. Just enough time to start our first singing group at St. Anne's parish. Love was new and exciting, and we were on our way to the adventure of our lives.

We moved back to Tucson because Enrique Loret de Mola finished his time with the army and he began getting his degree at the University of Arizona, God's school!

Our first 4.5 years were filled with family, friends, love, fights, faith; a broken ankle in Marana, Arizona; driving back and forth to Phoenix in an orange 1973 Volkswagen Bug, a first dog named Prima, Henry's graduation from God's school in 1979, and the beginning of our family... Nicolas (yes spelled without the "h") Enrique Loret de Mola. Oh, how we couldn't wait to be parents. Shortly after finding out we were pregnant, Henry took a position with EDS. Electronic Data Systems. His first position moved us to New Jersey...Linden...to be specific. As Stew Kanzler (Katie's little brother) would say, GOD'S COUNTRY!

Nicolas was born in Rahway, NJ, and we lived in Linden for about seven months or so. I was four months pregnant when we settled there.

Henry worked in New York City...Manhattan. He took a train every day back and forth. The cost of living was outrageous, and living on fourteen thousand dollars a year was not easy! But we managed, and soon Henry rose to another position as we moved to Downingtown, Pennsylvania. The memories of Downingtown are so special and wonderful. My friend Pam still lives in PA, and we keep in touch. We started a teen singing group there at St. Joseph's Parish, which lasted only one Sunday...even though we practiced for weeks. The pastor was furious with me because we sang the "Our Father." And that was that. We had Nick baptized there, and we changed parishes.

Yeah...you don't look back when a priest threatens to have you arrested if you ever sing in HIS parish again. My faith continued even stronger after that humiliating experience. What doesn't kill you...makes you stronger!

Two years after Nicolas was born, our second joy came...Alexander Tomas. Nick wasn't too sure about Alex. Mom and Dad came each time we were close to giving birth. Dad wasn't able to stay as long because I seemed to always go two weeks longer than my due date. Mom came to stay with us. Nicolas put two and two together...Grammy came, and Alex showed up. A week after having Alex, Mom had to get back to Phoenix. We all got into the bug for the drive to the Philadelphia airport. How did we manage that one? Who knows?

In 1981 we were able to walk Mom to the plane as she boarded. None of us will ever forget what Nicolas said to Gram as she cried as she walked up the ramp to board the plane. Nick realized something was different and yelled... TAKE ALEX. TAKE ALEX! Grammy showed up, Alex showed up...so he must be hers! Oh my gosh! I still smile thinking of that precious moment!

We lived in PA for four years and truly loved the state. We weathered snow for the first time, and I even went to work at a hospital, in cardiology. I loved it. Great memories.

Next came a move to Plano, Texas. We lasted three months in Plano, but EDS had plans for Henry in Bonham, TX, so...off we went.

I think we lived in Bonham for a year or so. Not my favorite place. But we got involved and sang at church with our sons close by. And soon I was pregnant with Franko.

About a month before I delivered, Henry was given another position, and we moved to Garland, TX. This was nice because we lived fairly close to my sister, Tricia. Thank God for Tricia because she was able to help me get her OB-GYN, and I delivered Frank a month after moving to Garland. Crazy time! Mom came again, and I remember watching her give Frankie his first bath in the kitchen sink at the house we rented. That memory is ever more special now to me.

We lived in Texas for about another year, and Henry was sent to Michigan...Sterling Heights became home.

We LOVED Michigan! We started a singing group at St. Matthias, and we made lifelong friends with the Zalar Family and Pat Berg and family. I made my best friend there, Kathy McCormack, and we shared kids and lots of laughter!

My next-door neighbor Linda Arvo was my lifesaver at times, and I still keep in touch with her and her daughter Heather. Life was so wonderful there that we knew it was time to have another baby. And so, God blessed us with our son number four…David! He was such an easy baby, and his brothers loved him. So much love in our home and great friends helped when we longed for family in Arizona!

After Michigan, there was our incredible move to Sacramento, then New Hampshire, then back to Sacramento. There is so much more, but I am boring myself. Suffice to say, I WOULDN'T CHANGE A SECOND OF ANY OF THIS…except for our great loss last September. Even in that, faith has grown for me. And love continues.

Enrique Loret de Mola, I am not me without you. You complete me. You are my patient rock and loving husband. I thank God for all He gave us, especially our sons, and now our grandchildren. How blessed are we. How thankful I am for you!

I love you!

Me

4/13/18

I struggle with things in my life…Is this God's will?…Is that God's will. Did God have a divine plan for Frank? Was this God's will? I believe God didn't want our son to die, but because Frank died, God opened Heaven's gates and let him enter with bells on his toes and songs coming from his heart. I believe the divine plan for all of this is yet to be revealed, IF I open my heart. THAT is the hard part. I need to sit back a bit and allow God in. His WILL be done. Alleluia!

Gus Lloyd speaks beautifully about this thought…Thanks again, Gus! You help my journey in faith!

"If It Is of God ..."

"For the next week, our Gospel readings will be from John 6. It starts off today with Jesus feeding five thousand with just five loaves and two fish. In the first reading from Acts 5, a wise rabbi addresses the Sanhedrin about the Apostles and these new followers of the Way.

"Gamaliel says, 'For if this endeavor or this activity is of human origin, it will destroy itself. But if it comes from God, you will not be able to destroy them; you may even find yourselves fighting against God.' This certainly became prophetic for the Church.

"Have you ever struggled with God's will for you? I think we all have. And I think Gamaliel's words hold true in many areas of our lives. God puts a desire in our hearts for a reason. Sometimes we just have to give it a shot and see if it's from God. If it goes south, maybe it was from God but was preparing you for something else. My point it this: If you have a passion for something, follow it and see what God wants to do with it.

"Father, help us to remember to put everything into your hands, and give us good discernment to know whether our endeavors are from you. Amen."

More

Home...getting gas...Back to reality. Just don't like reality sometimes.

We stopped to get the police report since we were driving that direction. Nothing new...Frank's gone. Nothing is going to bring him back. And we are home. Did I say that?

Another moment in time...

I love you, Enrique Loret de Mola. Thank you for loving me and all of our beautiful family.

Thank you for our time to just be!

4/15/18

Franko and LJ:

LJ, Louie James Hilario, shared this picture of when he and Frank Loret de Mola went back to Sac State and revived "Beans and Rice." They were so much fun to listen to when they had their radio show.

This morning I opened Facebook, and this picture took my breath away. I cried…of course…but I smiled knowing how much fun they had and how many people enjoyed listening to their antics. Another reason I miss you, Son! But so thankful for your giving life, and you will remain in our hearts!

I know I have shared this picture already, but it is worth sharing again!

4/16/18

We all go through this gift called life differently. We enjoy it, laugh, weep, sing because of it, mourn, and rejoice, but it is our way…our life.

I mourn differently than Enrique Loret de Mola. His hurt is no bigger or lesser than mine. Frank Loret de Mola's brothers mourn in their way…different from me…no more, no lesser…I tend to be verbal…or at least I write.

My heart is aching again. Maybe it is because a few of us sang for a double funeral today…I believe that is why my heart is aching. My beautiful friends, Nancy Tran and Carlota Agard, went to lunch with me, and it truly helps to lessen the hurt. But I have to stop eating out! Seriously not good for the weight. But I love the time together.

I came home to the quiet to think about a friend who lost her sister on Good Friday unexpectedly and her mother on Holy Saturday...kind of expected. I feel the deep sadness but also the joy for Julia because her faith is so strong. She knows what eternity is and her belief in the hereafter is palpable. But that doesn't mean it is easy.

Frank is right with me. Always will be. And eternity is just a number. Someday I will know what that is all about too. Until then, I will hold my loves close and my God closer! Amen!

4/17/18

Gus Lloyd's reflection on today's reading from Mass. This is the very reason I remain Catholic. I believe in the tran·sub·stan·ti·a·tion, the bread and wine becoming the body and blood of Jesus. This is difficult for those who don't understand...and I honestly understand and appreciate what I receive. But truthfully, it took me almost sixty years to really get it! And now that I do... wow! I thank God for this amazing grace!

Gus Lloyd:

"What Sign?"

"In today's first reading from Acts 7, we read about the martyrdom of St. Stephen. The last line of today's reading says, 'Now Saul was consenting to his execution.' There's a great scene in the new movie *Paul, Apostle of Christ* that has to do with St. Stephen. (You should see it.)

"We continue in John 6 and the Bread of Life discourse in our Gospel reading. The people ask Jesus, 'What sign can you do, that we may see and believe in you? What can you do?' Little did they know...

"Jesus was speaking of the Eucharist. He knew that in a very short time, He would give the world the greatest sign ever, and forever. His Flesh to eat and His Blood to drink. He has given the greatest sign, the greatest miracle in history. A miracle that will remain until He comes again.

"Father, so many miss the sign—the Body and Blood of the Lord. May we see it more clearly and share the message with all of the Holy Eucharist. Amen."

4/17/18

"It is not lengthy prayers, but generous deeds that touch God's heart."

— St. Arnold Janssen

4/18/18

Forgiveness is definitely a part of our lives...has to be! If not, how could I get through each day without Frank Loret de Mola? Not sure I could! Please be a forgiving, FRANKtitude kind of person!

4/19/18

Wow...

"The bread you store up belongs to the hungry; the cloak that lies in your chest belongs to the naked; the gold you have hidden in the ground belongs to the poor."

— St. Basil the Great

4/21/18

"Here is a rule for everyday life: Do not do anything which you cannot offer to God."

— St. Jean Marie Vianney

I posted this last year. Organ transplants have become something more to me than I could have EVER imagined at this time last year! Still so proud of the people of UCD Transplant Department! Thank you for all you do to make lives LIVE! My heart is so thankful! Polly Bleavins and Gina Pak Dela Cruz, this one's for you! Love to all who sign up to donate, who so generously give, and who gave their lives to others sacrificially! It takes a huge team of people to make this happen and change lives! Proud mom of a beautiful donor!

4/22/18

Seven months...still can feel the wind getting sucked out of my lungs, but I am also finding joy...I mean real joy! Missing my third son something fierce, but yet peace comes. Weird this thing called mourning. Roll with it!

4/23/18

It just happens...unannounced...unexpected...without any cause...I miss you, Frank Loret de Mola...Son. Your beautiful mind and soul are greatly missed. I continue without you. Sometimes I wonder how years will go by without you. Then other times I just pretend you are at work. Can you see me writing to you? Can you hear me call your name? Can you feel how much you are missed? I love you.

4/24/18

Our family wants to plan something special for Frank Loret de Mola's birthday on Saturday, July 21. Would love to also make this a donation opportunity to feed the homeless. David Loret de Mola suggested busking. I said... then open house at our home for all who knew and loved Franko. Ideas? Help? Kevin Seppinni wants to be a part. Of course, his girlfriend too! You can private message me with ideas. Or you can private message any of the family as we start getting our ideas together. Thanks!

4/25/18

"Since happiness is nothing other than the enjoyment of the highest good, and since the highest good is above, no one can be happy unless he rises above himself, not by an ascent of the body, but of the heart."

— St. Bonaventure

On our way to Stockton. Please let this be over, Lord! Please bless this process and all involved; us, the accused, the lawyers, the judge, family and friends who still love Frank Loret de Mola and forever will! Bring peace. Bring true forgiveness to all who can't forgive yet. Bring hope for a future without Frank. Let us send love to the heavens so Franko can feel it! I love you, Son! Pray for us...

More 4/25/18

Yes...my place with our sons is special and forever! Nick Loret de Mola, Alex Loret de Mola, Frank Loret de Mola, and David Loret de Mola...you have me, good or bad, in sickness and in health, when I piss you off, when I make you laugh (at me), when I love you and everything about you, and through the hardest times. I am proud to be the one who gave birth to you...

Okay...Dad was a huge part too. God was even bigger in all of it! I will always be thankful to be your Mom.

Michael Sanchez pleaded no contest to a misdemeanor, three years' probation and restitution. We are so thankful. No jail or prison! Praise God! Sentencing will be on May 15 at 8:30 A.M. We can speak then. Prayers have truly been answered. I said to him, please drive carefully now. He has been given an opportunity to start his life anew. God is in all of this, even in the pain.

Forgiveness is so healing.

Thank you for all prayers!

One more court hearing, and we will be able to move a few more steps ahead.

As I have said...this was a horrible accident, but to continue making anyone suffer more makes no sense...including suffering for Michael and all who love him. We all need forgiveness...some more than others...some more often than others...

Love to all! And thank you so much!

4/25/18 more

So many have said such nice things about how forgiving we are. Truly, forgiveness is something Enrique Loret de Mola and I have built our marriage on. You see, in forty-three years, there have been NUMEROUS times we could have held grudges, been mad for years, acted cruelly. But we realized months after we were first married that we needed to be able to say the words...I'm sorry. Please forgive me. I forgive you. I love you even if I don't like what you did...on and on.

I was raised in a big family. My folks had six of us. I remember my mom and dad making us kiss each other and say I'm sorry each time we would fight. We didn't like it...but we did it. I am thankful for that. Henry and I didn't make the boys kiss...but they had to say . . I'm sorry.

Forgiving takes the wrong done out of my head. I release the wrong and forgive the person who caused hurt. I have forgiven people many times in sixty-two years, and I believe I am healthier because I can forgive. Heck...I KNOW Henry should have dumped me YEARS ago...but forgiveness has kept us loving each other completely.

Please understand...I KNOW it is not easy. I forgave Michael Sanchez long before I knew the details. What good comes of unforgiveness? Who does it help? No one. Who does it hurt? Everyone!

I took to heart his girlfriend's word...FRANKtitude...or...What would Frank do? Live love. Live forgiveness. Live FRANKtitude. Be healers. Be peace.

I am a work in progress, and I know there will be days I question forgiveness...but not over this.

4/26/18

"Let us stand fast in what is right and prepare our souls for trial. Let us wait upon God's strengthening aid and say to him: 'O Lord, you have been our refuge in all generations.'"

— St. Boniface

I can be loving and accepting of others. I may not agree at all with you on different things. However, I truly hurt when my beliefs are mocked, made fun of, blasphemed, insulted, and when there are purposeful attempts to ruin the name of God, Jesus, the Holy Spirit, Mary the Mother of Christ, and any and all Saints and Angels. To laugh at people of faith is bigotry. To mock people of faith is prejudice. I am putting this out there for all to understand: This Jesus person I believe in is more alive to me and real to me than any other force in this world. Don't try to get to me with negative talk making fun of my beliefs. If my beliefs are not real to you, then why talk about them? They should be non-existent to you...so you should have no need whatsoever to speak of the God I ADORE. Quickest way to get unfriended...just saying...

4/27/18

Yes...I need to always remember this...

> "Help me to journey beyond the familiar and into the unknown.
> Give me the faith to leave old ways and break fresh ground with
> You."

— St. Brendan

4/28/18

Save the date...Saturday, July 21, Frank's birthday. Doing something, maybe a few things, to honor our beautiful Son. Will let people know more once we finish planning!

When Franko died, I was so very vulnerable. I barely remember the first few weeks, and to think, I even went to Tucson and JERUSALEM! Memories come back, but I don't think I'll remember everything about the first two months after Frank died.

Why am I saying this? I did things that were out of the ordinary to me. I asked so many people to friend me without a thought of how their issues and lives could affect me. I felt so much pain as well as happiness for total strangers. We had Frank in common or David in common. But I realized I just can't keep that going. I became overwhelmed, rightly so.

Today I felt awful unfriending people, but if they really want my friendship, I figure they will contact me...not me contacting them.

I love keeping in touch with my family and friends...Thank you for all the support the past seven months and even more...FOR MY WHOLE LIFE! All is good. All for the love of my sons.

Thanks!

5/2/18

MEDITATION OF THE DAY

"When it comes to explaining the Blessed Virgin Mary, having a lot of love is more important than having a lot of answers. When we come up lacking, she'll make greater goods out of our deficiencies, as only a mother can do. Whenever we're humiliated and shown our weakness, we should get ready for something better than we could ever plan and prepare to accomplish. Evangelize with joy, then, and with confidence. Know from the start that you don't have all the answers—but your Savior does, and He loves His mother. He will give you everything you need, even if sometimes you need to fail."

— Scott Hahn

VERSE OF THE DAY

"But I say to you that listen, love your enemies, do good to those who hate you, bless those who curse you, pray for those who abuse you...Give to everyone who begs from you; and if anyone takes away your goods, do not ask for them again. Do to others as you would have them do to you."

— Luke 6:27-31

More 5/2/18

Awake....

Why, Lord?

I still want to know WHY!

5/3/18

"Nothing great is ever achieved without much enduring."

— St. Catherine of Siena

I hope, in the end I endure. I believe I will! Please God!

5/4/18

"If we wish to make any progress in the service of God, we must begin every day of our life with new eagerness. We must keep ourselves in the presence of God as much as possible and have no other view or end in all our actions but the divine honor."

— St. Charles Borromeo

5/8/18

I am awake again. When I wake up it is usually this time of the night…two-thirty-ish.

Since Franko's death I have begun realizing this is God's time to get me to really pray or be still and listen. I sometimes hear the small voice in my head…Is it You, God, or my conscience making me think about words spoken or actions taken? Sometimes I realize something about myself I need to work on. Often, I just need to thank God for my life. Yes…I have begun to thank God for my suffering over the loss of Frank Loret de Mola.

People I love and I know have talked about the huge impact Frank made while on Earth. I believe, as my friend Pamela Pulido said, Frank's impact is even greater now. I believe he is able to help us more now because his essence can be felt by many more at the very same time.

What Frank gave to us, the wisdom he shared, is remembered and thought of simultaneously by many. If he were here, would all he gave be remembered as often? I don't think so because we would all just live life knowing we would see him tomorrow and kind of take for granted this incredible voice of love. But in his passing, our memories become so clear, and we remember more words he spoke to teach us. We remember the funny things he did with more clarity. We remember the love he shared, and we can all do that at the VERY SAME TIME and all have different thoughts about the very same person... Frank Loret de Mola.

You see, he IS doing his work still. He IS giving back to us. He IS still here in the remembrances of what he was all about: love, wisdom, truth, silliness, music, and peace. And so much more. Think of Franko as a gift we can all share now at the very same time!

Frank will never be gone because he is in my heart and yours. Take those quiet moments when you wake up and wonder why, and just cherish friendship and family gone before us who gave so brilliantly to our lives. Cherish the memory of Frank. I do. I cherish you too!

Love, Mom

"Have caution in not allowing yourself to be struck down by adversity nor becoming vain by prosperity."

— St. Clare of Assisi

5/9/18

Before Frank died and after Frank died is how I think now.

I have prayed all my life. I know I have gone through MANY times I ignored God, my faith, and anything to do with prayer, and turned my back on God.

After Frank Loret de Mola died, I have found an abundance of grace, and prayer comes easily. I find myself saying, "Good morning, Father!" Good Morning Mama Mary!" "Good Morning Franko" almost every day. I say good night often too, if I don't konk out too fast.

I have screamed at God, asking "WHY?" I have cried inconsolably, as I miss our Son with a passion that is indescribable. But I have also found great peace as I believe my prayers for comfort have been heard. I asked our

Blessed Mother to hold Frank in her arms and continue to ask of her. I believe I am heard.

I have groped for God (as Gus Lloyd shares today). I have begged for His help to understand all of this. I will never understand... but I will accept His will through ALL of this life-changing event. Lord, let this deepens my faith in You and strengthen me for the rest of my life's journey! Amen

Gus Lloyd's reflection:

"God is Always Near"

"Today in our first reading from Acts 17, we see Paul giving one of his great speeches, this time to the Greeks in the Areopagus. More on his message in a moment. In the Gospel reading from John 16, Jesus speaks of the Holy Spirit, telling the Apostles, 'But when he comes, the Spirit of truth, he will guide you to all truth.'

"Paul had seen an altar inscribed, 'To an Unknown God.' Paul seizes the opportunity to tell his Greek listeners about the one true God, who made heaven and earth. He says to them, 'so that people might seek God, even perhaps grope for him and find him, though indeed he is not far from any one of us.' I love the word used in the New American translation of 'grope.' I sometimes feel, in my life, as though I am groping for God. Those times when all seems dark and you know that God is around somewhere, you just can't seem to find him in the darkness.

"Paul tells his listeners that indeed, God is not far from any one of us. It is sometimes very hard for us to remember that God is always near. I think that even during those times where we drift away from God, He remains near to us. It's just that our backs are turned, or we're just not looking for Him at all. And when we are seeking Him but just can't seem to find Him, it is our lack of vision. So often we cannot see through our own woundedness. We can be blinded by our pain. But rest assured that God is always near. Sometimes you just gotta grope for Him.

"Father, thank you for always being near to us. Help us to open our eyes to see you more clearly, especially in those times where we are blindly groping for you. Amen."

5/10/18

I am waking up at what used to be my early bird time. I begin my day thanking God for another day and talking to Him. I love talking to Him. And I greet Mary our Blessed Mother. And I always say hi to my son, Franko. I know he is praying for all of us. I can see Frank, in my mind's eye, learning, listening, and watching. His knowledge now is immense. His understanding is beyond what we can comprehend. And I believe that.

Gus Lloyd explains the importance of today. The church celebrates many milestones of the Savior's life, but today is very important. Yes, these are human-made dates, but remember, to God there is no such thing as time. So today is a day we will really celebrate on Sunday, as a community, to remind us of the fulfillment of prophecies for proof to nonbelievers that Jesus is the One we all have waited for. The "Way, The Truth, and The Life".

Gus Lloyd:

"The Importance of the Ascension"

"Today the Church celebrates the Feast of the Ascension. In most dioceses around the country, today is not a Holy Day of obligation. For most, this feast will be celebrated this Sunday. If you are in a diocese or archdiocese where the Holy Day of obligation has been retained, you get to go to Mass today!

"The Ascension may be the most under-celebrated feast of the Church year. But the Ascension is vital to our faith. Why? Well, first let me quote Pope Benedict XVI. He writes, 'The meaning of Christ's Ascension expresses our belief that in Christ the humanity that we all share has entered into the inner life of God in a new and hitherto unheard-of way. It means that man has found an everlasting place in God...we go to heaven to the extent that we go to Jesus Christ and enter into him.' In essence, Christ's bodily ascension is the model for our spiritual ascension.

"The Ascension also opened the door to the Holy Spirit's coming. Remember, in John 16:7 Jesus said, 'For if I do not go, the Advocate will not come to you. But if I go, I will send him to you.' You see, Jesus could have stayed and ruled forever on the earth. But that was not the Father's plan. The sending of the Holy Spirit was the fulfillment of God's plan. And not just some old blueprint stuffed away in some file cabinet. But God's plan for your life. Jesus told his disciples to rejoice that He was going. And so today should be a day of rejoicing for us. So, rejoice! Jesus has taken His place at the right hand of the Father!

"Father, we thank you for the Ascension of our Lord, who now sits at your right hand. Let us rejoice, knowing that the time will come when we, too, will join Him with You in heaven. Amen."

I love this scripture. It calls me to prayer.

VERSE OF THE DAY
"The eyes of the Lord are on the righteous, and his ears are open to their cry. The face of the Lord is against evildoers, to cut off the remembrance of them from the earth. When the righteous cry for help, the Lord hears, and rescues them from all their troubles. The Lord is near to the brokenhearted, and saves the crushed in spirit."

— Psalm 34:15-18

5/11/18

Gus Lloyd has shared great reflections this week. I understand pain. You understand pain. How can I find joy in all of this? By God's grace.

I find joy in the small things in life more than I used to.

Joy comes in the baby at a restaurant the other day. I said, "Hi beautiful girl!" She lit up! Joy! I find joy in roses blooming in my backyard because of a gift of love. I find joy in the eyes of Enrique Loret de Mola, who comes home today after a week of business. I find joy hearing David Loret de Mola speak his truth to people about his life. I find joy in walking in the cool morning, even if allergies are awful! My grandchildren just have to show up, and I find joy! Too many other ways to mention!

The point is... no pain can keep me from joy! I trust this process!

Gus Lloyd:

"Faith and Childbirth"

"In today's first reading from Acts 18, Jesus comes to Paul in a vision and tells him, 'Go on speaking and do not be silent, for I am with you.' Words to live by, my friend. In the Gospel reading from John 16, Jesus analogizes the Apostles faith journey with childbirth.

"Jesus says, 'You will grieve, but your grief will become joy. When a woman is in labor, she is in anguish because her hour has arrived; but when she has given birth to a child, she no longer remembers the pain because of her joy that a child has been born into the world.'

"As men (and as a man myself), they could not fully understand that concept. But grief or pain becoming joy is certainly one that we can wrap our heads around. On our faith journeys, there will be times of great pain. But pain gives way to healing—physical and spiritual—which brings great joy. As we grow in faith in Christ, we'll think less about the painful things and concentrate more on the graces and blessings from God. Let's work on that today.

"Father, help us to let go of pain, no matter how long we have hung onto it. May we rejoice in the good that the pain has brought into our lives. Amen."

"Put your heart at His feet. It is the gift He loves most."

— St. Elizabeth Ann Seton

5/12/18

"Occupy your mind with good thoughts, or the enemy will fill them with bad ones. Unoccupied, they cannot be."

— St. Thomas More

5/12/18

I used to say Mother's Day was no big deal. That changed on September 20, 2017. It IS a big deal. My heart hurts today...again!

5/13/18

This week mercy will be shown.

"For there are three ways of performing an act of mercy: the merciful word, by forgiving and by comforting; secondly, if you can offer no word, then pray—that too is mercy; and thirdly, deeds of mercy."

— St. Faustina Kowalska

Wow!

MEDITATION OF THE DAY

"We will never be free of trials and temptations as long as our earthly life lasts. For Job has said: 'Is not the life of human beings on earth a drudgery?' (Job 7:1). Therefore, we should always be on our guard against temptations, always praying that our enemy, the devil, 'who never sleeps but constantly looks for someone to devour,' (1 Pet 5:8), will not catch us off guard. No one in this world is so perfect or holy as not to have temptations sometimes. We can never be entirely free from them. Sometimes these temptations can be very severe and troublesome, but if we resist them, they will be very useful to us; for by experiencing them we are humbled, cleansed, and instructed. All the Saints endured tribulations and temptations and profited by them, while those who did not resist and overcome them fell away and were lost. There is no place so holy or remote where you will not meet with temptation, nor is there anyone completely free from it in this life; for in our body we bear the wounds of sin—the weakness of our human nature in which we are born."

— Thomas á Kempis, p. 31, *Imitation of Christ*

5/14/18
I absolutely LOVE this quote!

"Heaven is filled with converted sinners of all kinds, and there is room for more."

— St. Joseph Cafasso

I love my faith and this quote from St. John of the cross helps me understand better, why!

MEDITATION OF THE DAY
"The reason why the soul not only travels securely when in obscurity, but also makes greater progress, is this: In general the soul makes greater progress in the spiritual life when it least thinks so, yea, when it rather imagines that it is losing everything...There is another rea-

son also why the soul has traveled safely in this obscurity; it has suffered: for the way of suffering is safer, and also more profitable, than that of rejoicing and of action. In suffering God gives strength, but in action and in joy the soul does but show its own weakness and imperfections. And in suffering, the soul practices and acquires virtue, and becomes pure, wiser, and more cautious."

— St. John of the Cross

5/14/18

Last year… I love you Frank Loret de Mola! Wow! Didn't expect this. Oh God! From Franko in 2017:

"Happy Mother's Day to all the mothers out there! Jackie Loebe put in a lot of time on this one. Hope you had fun today."

More…

Seeing a Mother's Day post from Frank Loret de Mola from last year took me by surprise and tears are flowing. I am alone and it is my time…Me and God have some talking to do! I WANT FRANK BACK! I know that can't happen, but I really do! Tomorrow is huge for us. Please pray for all of us: his girlfriend, and David Loret de Mola, Enrique Loret de Mola, and me as we share what losing Frank has done to our lives. Someday I will be able to say Frank's name with fewer tears. But for now, I am allowed. If I offend you or you think I need to get over it… well…sorry. I am a mother deeply mourning a child so loved and needed in our family.

In time, with God's love and help, I will get better. For now, allow me to wail and scream and cry harder than I ever knew possible. And pray for us to figure out a new way of life without Franko!

I needed this before I sleep. My pain is really about love. If I never loved my four sons, then I would not be in so much pain at the loss of one. BUT… I KNOW LOVE! I LIVE LOVE! And by George…I am love.

I thank God for pain because all it means is that I truly love! I love so much it hurts...so good! Then love away, but be ready for the pain, because when it comes, it is real! And welcome love and let it in. And let it become you, and let it become me. And never ever stay far from love! Let it bring you and me to our knees in thanksgiving for love.

5/15/18

MAY 15, 2018

"Have patience with all things, but chiefly have patience with yourself. Do not lose courage in considering your own imperfections, but instantly set about remedying them, every day begin the task anew."

— St. Francis de Sales

5/15/18

On our way to the sentencing right now. Hard day. But by God's grace we will rise to show who Frank Loret de Mola was and is to our family! I want the world to know what an incredible man he was! His death takes on new meaning today. Michael Sanchez is forgiven, and he needs to understand that his actions were a part of a bigger problem in our world...a lack of thinking of others and our split-second decisions can bring untold sadness. However, my hope is in a God whose forgiveness is far bigger than anything I can possibly do!

"Have patience with all things, but chiefly have patience with yourself. Do not lose courage in considering your own imperfections, but instantly set about remedying them, every day begin the task anew."

— St. Francis de Sales

5/15/18 11:32 A.M.

Okay…it's over. We said our impact statements. We heard the cries not only from our mouths and hearts, but from Michael too. He is so sorry. He told me several times. He gave me a Mother's Day card. He is…he just is…no words needed.

We are done with this part. Now time to trust God for our future of hope and a bright tomorrow. Frank lives forever in our memories. Frank lives forever in my heart and in my deepest soul. St. Frank Loret de Mola, pray for us!

For all who are hurting over our beautiful Son's death, you are in my prayers and held tightly in my heart. Let's move forward together!

Peace be with YOU!

With love and thanksgiving,

Jackie Loebe Loret de Mola

5/15/18

Mark Hart:

"On the final day of your life you won't regret all the times you spent in prayer… but you will regret all the time you didn't."

More…

Relaxing…much needed.

I thank God for this day. It was much harder than I imagined, but there is a sense of relief. Franko would be proud of his family and partner. I believe FRANKtitude played a huge part in all of the outcome, but my Savior is the reason for the outcome! Lots of prayers were said, and I believe God saw the goodness in those prayers and granted our petitions.

I have to say, I don't always get the answers I WANT, but I always get answers I need…even if the answer is ABSOLUTELY NO! I still thank God, even in the "No"!

Thank you to everyone for all your beautiful prayers for our family and his girlfriend. Thank you for understanding me when I just couldn't do any more or when I quit doing things. God knew I needed time and still do!

Your prayers are what kept me going, even when I was so low, I couldn't look up to see down! And that has been a struggle, but I will heal no matter what! I have to! I WILL!

God be with all! My love to all!

The journey continues!

5/15/18 10:00 P.M.

I thank God this day is almost over! I dreaded this day, yet I welcomed it. In time, today will be a blurry memory, but Frank will be forever in my heart.

I will move forward in time.

If anyone would have shown me ahead of time that we would lose one of our sons, I would have made sure to beg for it to be me and to trade places. I still would. I can't change facts. No miracle happened. No resurrection happened. But the blessings are many, and I am thankful for my incredible family and friends that prove to me, God is in all of this!

Goodnight all. When I say I love you, I mean it! You should all know that by now!

5/16/18

Today's quote is SO perfect!

> "I have been all things unholy; if God can work through me, He can work through anyone."
>
> — St. Francis of Assisi

5/16/18

I am going to share my impact statement I read yesterday. I don't want any comments because they don't matter. It is my heart, and I believe Frank Loret de Mola is pleased with the outcome of all of this. It is long… I could have said even more. Written with so much love,

Words to Michael Sanchez:

5/15/2018

"When I found out Frank was in an accident and he didn't call me to say he was okay, I knew it wasn't good. On our way to San Joaquin General, Henry and I knew it wasn't going to be good. Being Frank's parents, we just knew. I felt it was bad. We prayed a rosary, but we felt his soul had already left. Sadly, I believe we were right.

"When I saw Franko, it made it so hard to believe it was real because he had no cuts or visible bruising. He looked beautiful. He looked like he was sleeping, so when the trauma doctor said there was nothing they could do, I couldn't hold back my crying and screaming. I have cried and screamed many times since. But I believe in eternal life and that comforts me.

I wanted to know what happened…Was the person drunk? Was the person on drugs? Was the person texting? I spoke with Sgt. Butler on September 21st and she informed me that there were no drugs, drinking, or texting involved. She was on the scene and saw Frankie. She said the driver was recklessly driving. She said that the person would be charged with felony reckless driving, and if the worst would happen and if Frank should die, then it would be felony vehicular manslaughter. I said…but I am forgiving…WE are forgiving…She said…you have no say. It is the state against the defendant. I had no idea who you were, Michael. But in my heart, I knew this was a horrible accident. I knew you had no intention of killing my third son. But you did. It happened. All because you might have been in a hurry. All because you weren't paying attention and wanted to get home to your daughter and family. Whatever the reason, you changed our lives forever. But I forgive you. I know my Frankie would have wanted it that way.

You see, Michael. Frank Anthony Loret de Mola was a lover. He was a peacemaker. In fact, before his death, he was trying to help all of us come together in a family meeting to help us bury some old wounds. We had planned for many months that we would meet at our home on September 23rd. I watched our other three sons while we were at the hospital, holding each other, talking to each other, and what seemed like forgiving each other as we waited for a diagnosis and eventual decision to donate his organs to save others. Our family had been in pieces for several months, and Franko helped bring us together to meet...but that meeting never had to happen because he was taken from us the day before the meeting would have happened.

Michael, Frank was the person everyone wanted as a fiend. When he was little, moms would beg me to let Frank play with their sons because he was such a sweetheart. He knew how to be a great friend.

Believe me, Frank was not an easy child to raise. He wanted answers to everything, including belief in God. But he was someone who was the best friend anyone could have wanted...loyal and life-lasting.

He loved puns and could throw one out before anyone could think of a comeback. His laugh was contagious, and he was quick with a joke. His smile lit up a room, and he was always deep in thought trying to figure out how he could help the homeless, the children he tutored, and his nephew Jacob and family and friends who just needed help moving or an ear to listen. Oh, he was a GREAT listener.

He never had a real girlfriend until his girlfriend. He longed to have a family and children of his own. Our son Alex told me in the hospital, "Frank was so lonely, Mom," but he told me how happy he was that Frank had his girlfriend. I will never know if they would have had children, and that is almost unbearable.

Michael, Franko was brilliant. He majored in English, but he could have majored in calculus and higher math. He was an incredible writer, so his brilliance was on many extremes. He loved music and especially Bob Dylan. He saw through Bob Dylan's awful voice because he read his lyrics. Frank was a lover of words and was well known in Sacramento for his spoken word and poetry. He was a philosopher and minored in philosophy.

Frank helped Sacramento City Councilman Steve Hanson get elected, and Steve spoke at Frank's funeral...He said, "Sacramento will not be the same without him." We actually had a funeral...FOR OUR SON! We are supposed to go before our children! A funeral. How can that be? But I forgive you.

I forgive you not just for you...but for me. Putting you in jail or prison would have brought suffering for you, and that is not what I am about. I would have suffered knowing you were there because you are a young man with only twenty-three years behind you, Michael. You made a huge mistake, but it does not have to define who you are and who you will be. You are not the accident. You are not a bad person. You made a horrible mistake, and I pray it is your absolute last one. Oh sure, you will make mistakes in your long life ahead, but make this your last giant mistake. Learn from this. Let this be a start of a new life for you.

Place positivity in your path. If you have negatives in your life's journey, change that. If you are unforgiving toward someone, extend an olive branch. If you need motivation to finish your education, get going! Help get Highway 120 fixed so no other mother has to say goodbye to a piece of her heart way too soon.

I don't believe it was Frank's time to go, but God allowed it. He is God's now. So are you. Go with God to love and serve him and all those you come in contact with. Let this decision for leniency be an instrument of peace in your life. Never forget, but move ahead and go make your life GREAT.

GOD BLESS YOU AND BE WITH YOU ALL THE DAYS OF YOUR LIFE.

Jackie Loret de Mola

Frank's Mom

5/17/18

Wow! Posted a year ago! So much learning in almost eight months! Too much time already gone! Yet, does it really matter? YES! The spiritual growth that has changed my life is truly unbelievable. If I hadn't grown in faith over the past eight months, then where would I be? I have no clue.

But I do know where I am! I am deeper in love with the God who saves me DAILY! I am thankful more deeply for Enrique Loret de Mola, David Loret de Mola, Nick Loret de Mola, Alex Loret de Mola, Frank Loret de Mola, and all my family, especially my Mom, Laura Loebe, and all my gorgeous friends who have loved me even when I have said no to spending time together.

What I have experienced in the past eight months is a lifetime of lessons learned. No one ever said I'd go through this, but no one ever said I wouldn't.

I've truly learned to slow down and take this lesson one minute at a time. I never was good with patience, but boy, I have learned what it means to wait. I never was a person to wait, but there truly is grace in the wait and waiting!

So...another beautiful morning of memories gone, and more to be made.

Going to take time to go to Tucson and enjoy my mom before a trip to Disneyland to enjoy a baby to be born...a friend's granddaughter soon to arrive!

AND THIS IS WHAT LIFE IS ALL ABOUT: LOVE...BIRTH...LOVE... LIFE...DEATH...RESURRECTION...ETERNAL LOVE!

Amen! And ALLELUIA!

A slide says...someday you will be just a memory. Be a good one. I shared that a year ago, 2017! Wow...Before Frank's death...

5/18/18

Wow! Was I being shown things before Frank's death? No! I was living life with exuberance and joy. I have always been mindful that life is short, but never in my wildest dreams would I have thought that reality would hit all of us as it has, FRANK.

There will always be things our children don't want to tell us. At sixty-two years old, I want my sons to know NOTHING is too big or too small to tell your dad and me. We love you and will love you NO MATTER WHAT! Being a parent IS the biggest opportunity in a person's life. It is wonderful and can be horrendous sadly. It is NOT a job! It is a vocation. It is the most important vocation! We bring life and love. Our children are our gifts given by God to take care of while they are on Earth. Until He gets them back. And He does get all of us back. Yes, He does. Even as I write that, I still have a very hard time grasping that reality.

So…take great care of the gifts we all have been given. Great care. Treasure our gifts. Hold our gifts with compassion and joy. Be a gift in return for our children. What we give will be given back to us in the form of grandchildren! How blessed are we!

I posted a year ago…

The hardest part of being a parent is watching your child go through something really tough and not being able to fix it for them.

Have faith. Trust God!

5/20/18

Okay…I posted this last year …think I need to stop posting things like this… I have ALWAYS been aware of MY OWN possible last days…NEVER EVER thinking of anyone else's. But…oh, how that has changed! A video that says, "Be happy. You never know how much time you have left." Posted 5/20/17.

5/21/18

"Love your enemies, do good to those who hate you, bless those who curse you, pray for those who mistreat you."

Luke 6:27–28, from *Our Daily Bread*

It's time to sleep. Asking for prayers for someone I love, and please continue to pray for those we love who have passed way too soon! It is eight months tomorrow that Franko died. I love you Son! Sleep with the angels!

5/22/18

Last year's post...another Wow!

Posted on May 22, 2017:

"See, my children, we must reflect that we have a soul to save, and an eternity that awaits us. The world, its riches, pleasures, and honors will pass away; heaven and hell will never pass away. Let us take care, then. The saints did not all begin well; but they all ended well. We have begun badly; let us end well, and we shall go one day and meet them in heaven."

— St. John Vianney
From *Morning Offering*

5/23/18

Wow! Gus Lloyd socks it to me today! Great reflection!

"What Your Life Will be Like Tomorrow"

"In today's first reading, St. James talks about tomorrow. Something we need to think about today. So, we will. In the Gospel from Mark 9, Jesus says, 'For whoever is not against us is for us.' These words of Jesus always remind me of the unity that we have with other Christians. After all, no matter where we go to church, are we not all 'for' Jesus? I sincerely hope so.

"St. James says, 'You have no idea what your life will be like tomorrow. You are a puff of smoke that appears briefly and then disappears.' Translation: tomorrow is not guaranteed. St. James puts a really interesting spin on this thought, putting it in a business setting, talking about making a profit. He tells his readers, 'Now you are boasting in your arrogance.'

"I'm a big believer in this concept. That's why I call my radio show "Seize the Day." It's okay to think about tomorrow, but never at the expense of today. Do we have our houses in order today? Is there healing that needs to be done today? Have you told the people you love that you love them today? If your tomorrow turns out to be eternity, how will you have left things today? What if today is your final tomorrow?

"Father, we thank you for today. Help us to make the most of our opportunities to love and serve each other so that, if You grant us tomorrow, it will be better. Amen."

5/24/18

"Reading the Holy Scriptures confers two benefits. It trains the mind to understand them; it turns man's attention from the follies of the world and leads him to the love of God."

— St. Isidore of Seville

VERSE OF THE DAY
"Ask, and it will be given you; search, and you will find; knock, and the door will be opened for you. For everyone who asks re-

ceives, and everyone who searches finds, and for everyone who knocks, the door will be opened."

— Matthew 7:7-8

More

I am in Tucson. Just for two weeks. I am loving being here again. I find a peace in Tucson. One I can't explain. Is it the mountains? Is it my family? Is it the desert? Is it my friends? Yes. It is.

Thanks for putting up with me the past eight months. My Facebook friends have come and gone. I probably turned family and friends off with my unending posts of sadness and all I've been going through. You are used to me being upbeat, constantly happy, rarely sad. Thanks for hanging in there with me. I get it if I've been too much. It's okay. I am not going this alone. I know that.

The journey of spiritual growth is rarely ever easy. I am fine. I am changed but still Jackie Loebe Loret de Mola.

5/25/18

"I place trust in God, my creator, in all things; I love Him with all my heart."

— St. Joan of Arc

5/26/18

MEDITATION OF THE DAY

"In times of spiritual coldness and laziness, imagine in your heart those times in the past when you were full of zeal and solicitude in all things, even the smallest. Remember your past efforts and the energy with which you opposed those who wanted to obstruct your progress. These recollections will reawaken your soul from its deep sleep, will invest it once more with the fire of zeal, will raise it, as it were, from the dead, and will make it engage in an ardent struggle against the Devil and sin, thus being restored to its former height."

— St. Isaak of Syria

More

The Old Testament clearly shows us the prophecies of Who is to come! Our Cornerstone. Our Rock. Our Lord! Alleluia!

VERSE OF THE DAY
"Therefore, thus says the Lord God: See, I am laying a stone in Zion, a stone that has been tested, A precious cornerstone as a sure foundation; whoever puts faith in it will not waver."

— Isaiah 28:16

More 5/26/18

I could NEVER walk this garden of life without the CONSTANT help of the Blessed Mother. I call her Mama and even Mom! Yes, I do.

The month of May is hers. Here is a little info about our Lady:

MONTH OF OUR LADY
"In addition to the myriad feast days honoring Our Lady under her many titles and virtues, the entire month of May is especially given to her praise. In the words of Pope Paul VI, May is 'a month which the piety of the faithful has long dedicated to Mary, the Mother of God...For this is the month during which Christians,

in their churches and their homes, offer the Virgin Mother more fervent and loving acts of homage and veneration; and it is the month in which a greater abundance of God's merciful gifts comes down to us from our Mother's throne."

VERSE OF THE DAY

"The fruit of the Spirit is love, joy, peace, patience, kindness, generosity, faithfulness, gentleness, and self-control. There is no law against such things. And those who belong to Christ Jesus have crucified the flesh with its passions and desires. If we live by the Spirit, let us also be guided by the Spirit. Let us not become conceited, competing against one another, envying one another."

— Galatians 5:22-26

More 5/26/18

"What we let into our minds shapes the state of our souls."

— *Our Daily Bread*

5/27/18

Working on something. Will take creativity and gumption. Will share more when I am ready. Yes, it will be Frank Loret de Mola related. Love to all! Prayers please!

5/27/18

Thinking of Frank Loret de Mola, which I do all the time. I wonder what he would be doing this long weekend. Seems he never had many of those. In fact, he would work on holidays because the stores would stay open. We love our coffee in this city. But sometimes…no let me be honest…all the time, I felt cheated! I wanted him to spend time with us, but he would say he would work so someone with kids could be off for their families. I get that, but I don't have to like it.

Frank was selfless. Not too many people are selfless, but our son really was. He exuded kindness to the point that he put aside any of his needs and wants to care for others. He lived for others, and life wasn't about him.

I am not and never could be Franko. I know I am selfish and can be high maintenance too often. Frank was extremely the opposite! I think I bugged him because I was so materialistic compared to him. That is a lot for me to say out loud, but it is true. And I am proud of that quality our son had! He was humble and lived humbly. He would give the clothes off his back if someone else needed them!

I miss Franko so much. I doubt that will ever change. And those of you who got so much time with Frank, you are so lucky! You have far more pictures than I do.

Henry and I had to understand that our son was not ours alone; he became one for all. I'm not lying, that was very hard. I wanted to see him on his birthday, but we usually saw him a few days before it or weeks later. I learned how to let that go. I never complained to Frank, but Henry knew it hurt. I'd get over it, especially when we'd talk on the phone. He sounded like he was smiling while talking to me, most of the time. I also could tell when he was sad or stressed, but I learned to not ask too much because he didn't want me to know, maybe so I wouldn't worry. I am his mom, you know, and sometimes some things are best left unsaid.

And I regret…that I didn't go to the roasting plant more! He was so busy, but if that was one way to see him more, I should have gone!

So my heart is a bit heavy tonight as I reminisce about our son. I'm allowed. I can almost hear you, Frank, saying…"Oh Ma! Stop it! It's all good!"

I love you. Thank you for being my son. I really miss you!

5/28/18 morning around 7:00 A.M.

This reflection from Gus Lloyd gets right to my soul! Am I willing to let everything and everyone go to follow Christ? Yes, but Jesus doesn't mean that...To me, He is saying... CHANGE MY HEART! Deeply change my heart and make Christ present daily!

Since September 22, 2017, I finally understood what it means to want to "lay down my life for a friend who happened to be my Son, Frank Loret de Mola! If I could have done ONE thing...I would have died to keep him alive! I would have traded places in a heartbeat. But God had other plans.

Gus Lloyd:

"Faith in the Possible"

"For our first reading today, we begin the first letter of St. Peter. Today we hear St. Peter reminds us that we will 'suffer through various trials.' But this suffering is not worthless. It will help us to 'attain the goal of faith, the salvation of your souls.' Thank God for suffering!

"Our Gospel reading today is from Mark 10. It is the story of the encounter between Jesus and the rich young man. You know the story. Jesus tells him that he must 'sell what you have, and give to the poor and you will have treasure in heaven; then come, follow me.' Of course, the rich young man couldn't handle this, so he went away sad. Jesus tells the disciples, 'It is easier for a camel to pass through the eye of a needle than for one who is rich to enter the Kingdom of God.' The disciples ask, 'Then who can be saved?' Jesus replies, 'For men it is impossible, but not for God. All things are possible for God.'

Of course, we know that this is true. After all, God is God. He can do anything. But we must always remember that God is not some kind of supernatural magician. We must be cooperators in God's plan for miracles to happen. Some would say that is not true. But the cooperation we must provide is simply faith. St.

Peter talks about faith in the first reading, calling it 'more precious than gold.' Yes, you know in your head that God can do anything. But do you believe with your heart?

"Father, give us faith. Faith to know in our heart of hearts that you can do anything. Heal us today, Lord; for with you, all things are possible. Amen."

5/28/18

Great day! Spent time with my beautiful friend, Annie Frias Mammen, and forgot to take a picture! Had a nice talk with a woman at Cracker Barrel about Franko and gave her one of the FRANKtitude bracelets I had made. She asked me about the necklace I was wearing. Sandi Austin gave it to me. It has a beautiful picture of Franko on it. She said she had a feeling there was a story behind it. So, we spoke for a while and hugged. Total stranger spreading love. Thank you, Son!

I got back to my mom's house and Auntie Yolanda Martinez was there ready to paint. Suddenly in came Yolie Cox, Deedee Van Balen, and Laura Hall—three of my cousins! Such a wonderful surprise and time spent together! I love my cousins. ALL of them!

I lay my head down feeling love for my family, who loves no matter what. I feel thankful for a day of happiness and joy. I am thankful for Enrique Loret de Mola because he loves me so much and never tries to change me! He lets me be in Tucson without any worries. I am blessed with my sons and grandchildren who put up with me needing my desert space. I know it seems selfish, but it is how I heal and survive. I need my mom still!

I am ready for another day.

Now I lay me down to sleep, I pray my Lord my soul to keep.

Guard me Jesus through the night and wake me with the morning light.

Angel of God my guardian dear to whom God's love commits me here.

Ever this day be at my side,

To light to guard to rule and guide.

Amen.

5/29/18

I'm in a breathless state right now. This song I dedicate to our sons and all of Frank Loret de Mola's friends. But it speaks from the depths of my being...Please listen! Beautiful, so beautiful! Some man singing on "The X Factor" that made Simon Cowell cry. Very moving!

Later at night:

Oh, I am missing you. It comes in strong waves, sneaking up on me. All it takes is to see your picture. The tears are flowing, and I beg God to take me to be with you. I beg Him to hold on to you to wait for me. Will it be another day or two? Maybe it will be forty more years. Please wait for me! We will hug each other again. Will you recognize your old mom?

I do fine. I do really, really fine, and then...like a horrible nightmare, all of it comes back. And crying is good. Sort of. I miss you as I lay down to end this beautiful day. Even though my thoughts are all about you, Frank, I know I have more to finish on this Earth. I need your dad and your brothers. I need them now more than ever. I need you too, Franko, but I will have to wait. And wait and wait.

Why? Why? Why?

5/31/18

The Meditation of the Day is deeply real for me! How can it be May 31, 2018 already? Frank Loret de Mola, I ache for you but I believe you are helping to find solutions to our world's unrest!

Be blessed my Son!

MEDITATION OF THE DAY

"What words, can, alas, express the deep grief of the Blessed Virgin? Her eyes closed, a death-like tint overspread her countenance; unable to stand, she fell to the ground, but was soon lifted up, and supported by John, Magdalen, and the others. She looked once more upon her beloved Son—that Son whom she had conceived by the Holy Ghost, the flesh of her flesh, the bone of her bone, the heart of her heart—hanging on a cross between two thieves; crucified, dishonored, condemned by those whom He came on earth to save; and well might she at this moment be termed 'the Queen of Martyrs.'"

— Bl. Anne Catherine Emmerich,
p. 29 of *The Dolorous Passion*

6/1/18

Gus Lloyd has given me food for thought. I really need to figure out my scriptural life verse.

I wonder if my life verse is from Job, who suffered so much as he lost his loved ones over and over.

I wonder if my life verse is from St. John because his writing is so deep and makes me think more deeply.

I wonder if my life verse is from Ruth…"Wherever you go, I shall go. Wherever you live so shall I live. Your people will be my people. And your God will be my God too. Wherever you die I shall die. And there shall I be buried beside you. We will be together forever. And our love will be the gift of our lives." Yes, that is my life's verse.

Thanks again, Gus Lloyd! I've got it, and I have had this as my verse for a very long time and now it makes way more sense!

Enjoy Gus's reflection:
"A Life Verse"

"Do you have a Life Verse? Do you even know what that is? A Life Verse is a passage of Scripture that you adopt for your own. A passage that speaks right into your heart; one that you try to live by, that guides your steps. The reason I bring this up today is because part of the today's first reading is my Life Verse.

"'The end of all things is at hand. Therefore, be serious and sober-minded so that you will be able to pray. Above all, let your love for one another be intense, because love covers a multitude of sins. Be hospitable to one another without complaining. As each one has received a gift, use it to serve one another as good stewards of God's varied grace. Whoever preaches, let it be with the words of God; whoever serves, let it be with the strength that God supplies, so that in all things God may be glorified through Jesus Christ, to whom belong glory and dominion forever and ever. Amen.' (1 Peter 4:7-11)

"If you don't have a Life Verse, I encourage you to start the process of adopting one. Pray it daily. Let it remind you of God's great plan for your life. Share it with others! If you like, feel free to use mine! Whatever you select, you can never go wrong with God's word in your heart.

"Father, may we always draw closer to you through your holy word. May your word lead and guide us at every stage of our lives. Amen."

6/3/18

My time in the desert of Tucson is almost over. The continued healing feels so good. Have I cried? Yes! Has my heart ached? Yes! Have I scream laughed? YES! Do I have more life ahead? Absolutely! And by the grace of God, this old mom will continue being blessed daily by the memories and the future that is on its way.

God blessed me with a husband who loves me unconditionally and who is my rock. I have been blessed to know this kind of love. Thanks be to God!

Our sons are each unique and incredible human beings. Each one brings so much to our family, and I can't thank God enough for the men they are.

I thank God for everything in my life—yes, even my greatest trials and heartbreak. Through it all comes so much understanding of what the human spirit can endure. LOTS! I am further into this thing called healing. I am ready to continue this journey.

God's got me!

6/4/18

I woke up today thinking about Frank Loret de Mola. What else is new? But this is a new thought; if Frank's Spirit was so strong when he was with us, what's keeping his same spirit from continuing?...ABSOLUTELY NOTHING!

I have said I ask Franko for prayer. How can I do that? Why do I do that?

I believe, from the moment of conception, everyone is given a soul. That soul is blessed by the spirit. How we choose to use that spirit is up to us once we can make decisions. Frank didn't always make the right choices, but neither do I. BUT—and this is the big thought—his spirit of choice for giving of his heart, giving of himself, giving of his patience, giving of his time, giving of his intelligence, giving of his hope for tomorrow, giving of his love and so much more, is still here! Yes, we all do those things in our lives, but some of us just know HOW to do that and do that VERY well! Frank was and remains to be that spirit.

So, when I see Henry and our sons and our family and friends, I see the spirit God gave them. I choose to be a Pollyanna and see the goodness and not the darkness. If and when I DO see darkness, I pray. I choose to be in the light. Join me...in the light.

So...I ask God permission to ask Frank for prayers for you and for me. I know Frank's positivity is even stronger now. He continues to affect my life and always will.

Seek positivity. Seek FRANKtitude. Seek your spirit, the Holy Spirit, Who is keeping me feeling hopeful and blessed to know that I choose to live in love.

Amen!

6/4/18 More

At night before I close my eyes, I talk with God. Tears came suddenly tonight, and I thought my crying would wake my mom. And then I asked God to let me feel Franko's presence. I asked for Mama Mary to take care of him again. I want to take care of him. I want to comfort him and be with him. But I can't. Why is it that the life after death is so hard on the living?

I believe I will see Franko again...in time. I want to see him again, on God's time...on God's time...

Sleep with the angels, my Son. I miss you.

I love you!

Mom

6/5/2018

"At the end of our life we shall be judged by charity."

— St. Paul of the Cross

6/6/2018

Shared on 9/18/2017...two days before Frank's accident.:

If we truly understood that God is mercy, our sin wouldn't make us run from Him, but TOWARD Him...

"To doubt forgiveness is the beginning of hell."

Fulton Sheen

6/8/18

I went on the ride, Soaring over the World, and I cried. It is such an incredible ride. Why the tears? Thinking of Franko and the things he didn't see. Ashley put her arm around me and comforted me. Needed that. Then Sandi and Maria said, "He's with you and sees it all now." I held on to the beautiful necklace Sandi gave me with Frank Loret de Mola's picture on it and felt he is saying, "Oh Mom, I'm here. I'm good!"

6/11/18

Why is it that when I come home, I sink into a sadness of longing for Frank Loret de Mola? It's like reality storms my brain, and my heart skips beats. Oh, how I miss you, Son! I love you!

From Kathleen, my sister:

"Jack...remember you are strong enough to face that reality head on. You have a family that supports you, and your faith in God carries you through. Reality sucks sometimes, but how we embrace it and work within it is what matters most. I love you so much and continue to lift you in prayer."

6/16/18

My friend Billie Pettit tagged me on this post. I listened, and the tears almost came again, but not from sadness. I had a hard time when I went to bed last night and again at 3:00 A.M.! Tears for Frank Loret de Mola flowed as I squeezed my pillow...as if squeezing my pillow would be like hugging him.

But then THIS! I want to believe this man. I want to believe Franko is sitting with others figuring out new music or discussing what God needs. I remember Frank telling me he wanted to be in a think tank! I bet he is!

The words from this writer calmed me and gave me daydreams of Frank just enjoying heaven and everyone there! I bet he's Mr. Popular! Oh my God, I miss him! Can't wait to see him again someday…in God's time, not mine…

My friend Billie Pettit shared the video that came with the reference below! Changed my sadness to hope!

What if one thousand people came back from death to confirm the Bible's exhilarating picture of Heaven? Book written by John Burke, *Imagine Heaven*.

Here is a perfect picture with words that describes me in my grief!

6/18/18

It is already halfway through June, and maybe that should make me happy. If I truly believe in eternity, then maybe I am a half month closer. Maybe not. If the goal of a faithful person is heaven, then we should all want to be there with hopeful anticipation. Then why does it hurt so much to lose family and friends? I know why! Because I am a human with only human understanding of the afterlife. But if it is half as good as it is promised to be, then we all should hope for each other to get there and soon. But I am no more ready right now than I was September twenty second. Another month almost gone without my son, Frank Loret de Mola. That's nine months. It took nine months and four days to give birth to him. It took one day to lose him. Yes, these are the things I think about as the night draws close. Missing his beautiful smile and puns! Missing his huge hugs! Just thinking of how busy he must be in heaven! Franko, pray for us! There is no religion there, just truth now, and that is all you ever wanted! I love you!

Mom

Later in the evening of 6/18/18:

I never ever want to forget you, Son, Frank Loret de Mola! How could I? You were growing inside of me, put there by the love of God and your dad,

Enrique Loret de Mola. And I thanked God then, and I thank God now for our family of five boys and one girl...Well...two girls counting Sheba. Your dad always said he was the fifth boy!

I am remembering your smile and your incredible laugh, Franko! Your brothers sound similar, but not quite, and I so don't want to ever forget your laugh! You kind of squeaked once in a while as you finished laughing! I love the memory of that!

Why am I teary now? I laughed so much tonight playing emoji tag with my sister Kathie Loebe. But now my heart aches because I want to see you again. NOW!

Okay...I will go to bed and sleep. I will walk in the morning and pray for you and your brothers and your dad and your recipients and Grammy and all the family and you again.

I love you, my Son! Be at peace!

6/22/18

Nine months gone. Wow! How can that be? Much of the past nine months is a blur. I know I have been living each day, but I can't believe how I got to today. I mean, I am still here even though I have begged God for me to trade places with Franko. Oh, I logically know that can't happen, but if it could...

So, THIS is my new normal, or whatever that is!

I truly am doing better...not crying as hard or as often. But I still have moments of breathlessness and sadness. The very thought that I won't see him for a long time just jerks me into reality.

I will probably always ask God why, but I am beginning to accept that Frank's time on Earth was over...WAY before it should have been.

I wonder...will I always write about Frankie? Will I ever find a time that suddenly it's been a year since I've written about our son? I doubt it! He, just like our other sons, are my life's story. I wouldn't be me without them. That is the truth.

And so, I am finding peace in this old life and thanking God for Frank's life because I know he really lived his life and continues to do the same giving of himself to this day!

Thank you, Son, for your giving life!

I love you!

Mom

6/23/18

A friend, Ann Dufour, posted this today. I saw it the other day and posted it then. I am sharing it again because I really get it! Never in my life did I think I would understand these words like I do now...but I do!

There's a picture with the words below on it:

> "Grief, I've learned is really just love. It's all the love you want to give but cannot. All that unspent love gathers up in the corners of your eyes, the lump in your throat, and in that hollow part of your chest. Grief is just love with no place to go."
>
> — Jaime Anderson,
> from lessonslearnedinlife.com

Henry responded to my post on Facebook of 6/22/18:

> "Yes, memories, what ifs, regrets, anger, fear of the unknown future of our sons, Jackie, and family... mind fissures flows that erupt unexpectedly...followed by acceptance, memories of Franko, and love that heals the burn...

6/24/18

This is a great reminder for me to ALWAYS keep God first! That can be so difficult sometimes when it is easier to ignore God's presence! He is real. As real as the new roses blooming in my backyard. God is as real as the songs sung to help a baby sleep. God is as real as the morning kiss from a loved one. God is as real as I want Him to be, and that is ALWAYS! After reality hits and all is stripped away from my consciousness, there God is...waiting for me as I beg For His love and forgiveness!

> VERSE OF THE DAY
> "And without faith it is impossible to please God, for whoever would approach him must believe that he exists and that he rewards those who seek him."
>
> Hebrews 11:6

6/26/18

Today the "Morning Offering" I received in my email is so beautiful! Each of us are saints "in the making"! We are all called to holiness, but not all of us believe that. I certainly don't see myself as worthy, but God's will is far greater than any of us can imagine. Here is today's "Morning Offering," and after you read that, I am posting my most favorite song sung by Hillary Scott. Her song brought me to tears today, after falling asleep with tears last night! I will share more after I post the song. My love for Frank Loret de Mola never ends. My ache is at the surface of my skin always!

> "MORNING OFFERING"
> "Dismiss all anger and look into yourself a little. Remember that he of whom you are speaking is your brother, and as he is in the way of salvation, God can make him a saint, in spite of his present weakness."
>
> — St. Thomas of Villanova

Last night I laid my head on my pillow. Henry was already sleeping. Tears fell and wet my face. I didn't want to cry, but it happened. Frank's face was in my eyes. I could almost touch him. But he wasn't there. I wondered how I was going to live without my son. I wondered if I could. Then the thoughts of Henry, Nick, Alex, David, Jacob, and Emma came, and I knew how I would survive this nightmare! I don't know if I will ever be "okay" with my life, but I will deal with this new way of life.

I am not the same person I was nine months ago. In some ways I'm better, more compassionate to the world around me and to the things going on that aren't in my control. I have reached a deeper level of my faith I never knew existed until I got in the midst of it. I see people with a different heart. Those are good things coming from this. And I also understand death a whole lot more! Yes, others I have loved deeply have gone, but THIS love...THIS one is a longing and aching and sadness that permeates me at times, and is all too real.

Enjoy this song! My favorite words she sings are, "Sometimes I've gotta stop, remember that You're God, AND I AM NOT! Thy will be done!"

Hillary Scott, "Thy Will Be Done"

A little while later on 6/26/18

MEDITATION OF THE DAY

"One of our sure guides along the path of life is that we do not know when earthly life will come to an end. How important that our repentance for past and present transgressions be a daily practice."

— Rev. Thomas J. Donaghy,
p. 36, *Inspirational Thoughts for Everyday*

Wow! A great reminder to live life to the fullest, always keeping God in the center! He watches us! He knows everything that is going on! He does see us! Am I making You proud, Lord? Or do I break Your heart? Forgive me when I deny You and turn my back to You! Please never let me go, Lord!

More 6/26/18

I was cleaning out my email folders and came across some old pics of Jacob at Jen and Nick's old rental. They totally took my breath away! I hear you, Franko! Yes! You will NEVER be forgotten! Oh God how I miss you! Yes, God! I am beginning to understand...a little!

This picture is of Jacob and Franko building with cups.

6/27/18

Yesterday was tough! I don't understand all the reasons I was so down, but I was hit HARD with tears for Franko. I guess those tears really are just love pouring out to the couch and cushions, so I can take one step forward today.

So...today I am better. Sort of in a "hangover" from yesterday. You see, the tears aren't surfacing today, but my heart needs to catch up to my emotions and stop racing.

I will ask for all of us to pray for love and God to be in our lives. I will ask Frank Loret de Mola to pray for brokenness and hurt, for health and pain, for peace and joy. Franko, please pray for us! Amen! And Alleluia!

My Jerusalem friend Kay Schmidt wrote back to me:

> "Hugs! Can't even imagine your pain. Prayers for your family. I admired so much that you went to Israel right after your son's death. I don't believe I could have done that...You are stronger than you know!"

6/27/18

David posted this:

> From Frank, before he passed:
>
> "You have to take care of the person.
>
> "No law passed will change that.
>
> "People who don't want to take care of others won't. People who want to take care of others will.
>
> "There isn't a policy that will pass to make people see each other as human beings.
>
> "There is no way to shirk off the responsibility we have to one another to treat each other fairly...It's a day-to-day thing. It comes with being less afraid of ourselves and the world.
>
> "Maybe embracing mortality is a good step. It has been for me. Makes all the smaller concerns and tensions less obtrusive.
>
> "I don't know. Get over fears, say something. Reach out.
>
> "No one can represent you. No one can govern you. Sure, people should control and regulate vital resources, and can regulate commerce, and levy taxes to do these things and maintain necessary infrastructure...
>
> "But no one can police your intentions. Or your neighbors'.

Open your eyes, acknowledge the realities of the people around you, and understand that all people want fundamentally the same thing.

"Often, the only reason we all disagree about how to get there is nurture through circumstance and environment.

"But think of what will bring any one person happiness, and it's the same story.

"Shelter, food, community, intimacy, something they take pride in doing.

"Want to convince people your position is right? Find out how they got to meeting those needs for themselves. Compare them to how you got to those needs.

"Then realize everything that doesn't relate to those needs are kinda made up frills that shouldn't impact anyone else's decisions, because they're only important to you.

"That often hurts and sucks.

"But then you can actually empathize.

"It's awesome and freeing, once you get there, because now you can spend half the amount of emotional energy you had worrying, fearing, and hating, and spend it doing something else.

"Just a process of thoughts, and a thought of processes."

6/28/18

Today I am realizing that maybe for me, putting one foot in front of the other is about all I can do right now. Tonight I am going to meet up with Debbie Berry Garcia and Twila Curtis Daly for dinner, and that will be so good for me! I walked this morning and took a bath. I am now resting, and tears keep coming. My cousin Dianne Miller texted me, and that is helping so much! God brings people into my life at the perfect time! Frank Loret de Mola, I LOVE YOU! I believe you can hear me in heaven! I really do! Another day... one foot in front of the other...one love and blessing from God. I'll be fine. I deserve this time and quiet as I also listen to my Christian music...Mercy Me! They are amazing!

7/3/18

I had a divine appointment today, unexpected and so incredible!

As I sit here just taking in what happened at the cemetery, where Frank Loret de Mola is... I am in awe of Gods mercy and grace!

Okay... so I have been super down for over a week, crying a lot, and wondering why! Frank's Birthday is July 21st, and as his Mom, I always reminisce about each of our son's births every year when they celebrate their birthdays. This year has hit me smack dab in my heart because Franko's birth was the hardest of all four, and not only that, when I was seven months pregnant with him, my life was threatened by a woman I worked with in Texas. It was awful, and I knew Franko was crying with me in my womb! I believe our bond truly was cemented at that time!

So anyway...I cried all the way to the cemetery, called my beautiful sister/friend, Kathy McCormack in Michigan, and sat in front of the cemetery crying and also laughing with Kathy. We hung up, and I walked to Frank's spot. Here's where it gets incredible!

As I was kneeling and praying and crying, I started to do a journal video of what I was feeling. I heard a car, I thought, but didn't see anyone. I finished the video, I think, and suddenly saw a woman getting ready to put flowers on a niche near Franko's. I said hi, and she said hi, and the conversation took on a life all its own, a divine appointment. Her husband is right near Frank. Her husband died in 2014, and her love is eternal!

I introduced myself, and she said her name is Maria. Her friends call her Ria. We talked about Franko and cried. We talked about her husband and tears gently fell. We shared a lifetime with each other in about forty-five minutes. She was beautiful. She was my angel for today and hugged me several times. We were sharing like two old friends who hadn't seen each other in years.

Only God could have put this together! Seriously! I needed her! She listened. I listened. Her husband sounded so wonderful, but of course he was! She was wonderful!

And now she has my phone number and I have hers. We might only see each other when we go to Pleasant Grove Cemetery, and maybe not. But I do know I walked away with a smile given by God's grace from a stranger who was placed in my path...My journey of faith!

Thank You, my God!

Thank you, Ria from Holland, who has been living in the U.S. For forty-nine years! Your purpose in this life helped this mourning, Mom! Thank you!

And...as I walked back to my car, I said, "Thank you! I am leaving with a smile on my face!"

7/5/18

I posted this some time ago, and it comes as I am reminiscing about all the sons I've given birth to, especially Franko. With each one, I always thanked God after they first came out to greet Enrique Loret de Mola and I. What glorious days those were.

Who would have ever understood the ups and downs, the joys and sorrows, that were in the future? No one could have ever prepared me for all our family has gone through. Way too much at times, for sure! If I could only take back the negative stuff and turn it into joy. But the truth is, it made me stronger in my faith. I leaned on God. That's how I have been able to deal with the toughest time yet! I will not abandon You, Lord! You never abandon me even when I scream at You and want to deny You. Like a good Father, you wait patiently for me to come back begging for You! Thank You, Father! Amen!

Under my writing is a sign that says: "Labor is the only blind date where you know you'll meet the love of your life."

7/6/18

I posted asking for Frank's friends to share with me anything about him, whether they've dreamt about him or have seen him.

Becky Kilgore, a.k.a. Rebecca August, wrote:

"Every time I see a "clubs" card symbol. There was a time right around when we all turned twenty-one when my ex-husband and I were at a friend's apartment for a TV show he'd go over and watch every week, and we were all joking around just having fun. Somehow Frank and I got into this ridiculous competition of making the worst drink we could out of everything in the fridge we could find. Frank convinced me he could telepathically make me guess what card in the deck he was holding, and if I guessed right, he would drink the combination of alcohol, juice, condiments, and milk on top (courtesy of his roommate, lol). I remember laughing hysterically and saying I had to be a good friend and not guess so that he wouldn't have to drink it. He laughed even harder and said a good friend would show the world his mind control skills. Long story short, I guessed the suit of the card was clubs , and he took one sip of the awful drink while laughing hysterically. To this day, I can't see any club card without smiling and thinking about that. That was one of those deep laughs where you have tears rolling down your face, and it's committed to memory. The rest of college, we'd usually say, "Clubs!" if we saw one another. I was thinking about it the other day while telling my husband that I pray our kids have friendships like that in their early adulthood. Frank was such a big part of one of the best time periods in my life."

I responded:

"My heart is sooooo happy! That is a GREAT story! Oh, my Son! He brought so much to so many!!!! He knew how to "friend"! When he was super little, moms wanted him to be friends with their kids. His outgoing nature, laughter, teasing, and so much more showed how much he cared about you! Oh My God, how I miss him! Keep remembering him! Thank you!

Carly Russell wrote:

"I really go through moments where I'm really very sad that he's no longer on this earth physically. But I think he reminds me to let live, let love, and enjoy all. In my moments of trying this year or when I was complaining, I am reminded how Frank was…and lightened up…like Franko the angel wings was like…I'm compassionate, but like hey, look what you have. But I'm really sad I won't see another post, hear a pun, or see how his life would have unfolded. I work daily to remember his laugh, the memories, and convos. I've had a few dreams this year. One of playing poker with all the college buddies with Frank. There was one recently where I told the new "replacement friend" in the dream that he could never really be Frank, because there isn't anyone like Frank."

I responded:

"Thank you, Carly Russell! You brought me joy hearing this! Thank you! I want to keep him alive in every possible way! You truly helped!"

Rachel Lickter replied:

"I think about him almost every day. I too long for his laughter and puns and for his wise advice."

I responded:

"Me too, Rachel! I need to come see you guys sometime. Just want to say hi and get a cup of coffee!"

7/7/18 more from previous days post.

A friend of mine from the Jerusalem trip, Brian Schmidt, wrote:

> "Never knew Frank but I wish I did after reading about him. He sounds like a great son. Hope each day the pain is less and the memory of him glows of happy times. Kay and I love you."

And I responded:

> "I love you guys! Thank you, Brian Schmidt! Thank you! He was amazing. Very human, but very special, as all our children are! Frank was charismatic and people easily wanted more of him! What he accomplished in his short lifetime, some of us couldn't begin to achieve even in 100 years! Thank you!"

7/11/18

Just placed a flyer about Frank's party on the community mailbox so the neighbors know there will be cars! I also had the opportunity to speak with Beatrice, our neighbor, to let her know. She lost two nephews within three months. She raised them. Tears in her eyes. We NEVER know what people are going through! Stay living and kind! Amen!

7/12/18

We never know how tomorrow will go. In a million years, I never ever thought we'd lose a child...EVER! Each day is truly special.

A friend lost her husband today. It was completely unexpected. When is death really expected? Never! Never!

I still have times I can't believe Franko is gone. But I also can't believe the death of so many friends who have died since Frank. It is just not right, but I have to try hard and find God in all of it! He is there, to lean on, for comfort, to hold you when tears can't fall enough, and to bring peace.

Oh, days are far too hard than we can ever imagine.

Love each other...NOW! It's all we've got!

7/13/18

Hard to believe how much has happened since this day last year. Life brings reality that is so hard to handle at times! When I find quiet and time to reflect, I now know God's hand was truly in all that happened on September 20th, Franko's accident date. God held him and gave him his way into heaven! I believe that with all my heart! Rest In Peace, my beautiful son!

7/16/18

This is a rough week! Marilyn Billinger and Ken, I know you understand! Franko would be thirty-four this Saturday. Today I got a Facebook Memory of him reading a book he received from my grandparents, his GREAT grandparents, when he was probably Jacob's age in the video. My prayers have been to hear Frank's voice again...and there he is! He really didn't change much since the video in 2011, but Jacob sure has!

I am asking for prayers not only for me, but for all of us who love and miss him so much! Henry, Nick, Alex, and David are hurting, and it is real.

What more can I say but, thank you! By the grace of God go I!

7/17/18

Today is thirty years since my grandfather, Frank Vasquez, passed. Our Frank Loret de Mola was named after Papa, and as far as I know, he was the only one named after Papa. What an honor, and Papa loved that!

Last night, when I woke up at around 2:30 A.M., I prayed, asking Papa for prayers and realizing Franko and his namesake were together. A peace came over me, and I knew they are probably playing canasta or something! What a journey this grieving has been!

God bless you, Papa, and kiss our Frankie for us! Can you show him your muscles?

I love my Franks!

7/18/18

True...I know I came from God. You may ask, come on, Jackie. How do you really know that? It is in the depth of my soul! My whole being blesses His Holy Name. When I cry out in pain and even anguish, I know I will take another breath, even if it is small and shallow. My life has been a moment by moment, sometimes a second by second encounter with God and His people. And I love this life. Thank You God. But I also know that loving God and trying my best for Him still brings the pain of losing a love...my child...our child. Frank Loret de Mola was not just me and Enrique Loret de Mola's child. He belonged to God.

I remember a day or two after my grandfather Frank Vasquez died, Henry and I heard clicking noises upstairs in our Michigan home. Frankie was sitting up in bed, a couple days before his fourth birthday, and he said, "His hands are big." Henry and I believed and still believe Papa came to say goodbye to Frankie. That is when I knew Franko was special and God had a plan for his life. I had no idea that it would be thirty-three short years.

You know, I don't talk about this much, but from the time I was in my teen years, I always believed I would never live through my thirties, and I always believed I would die in a car accident. Weird, huh? I think I understand why I always thought that...because I DID die. Not me physically, but my heart, and it wasn't about me! I think God allowed me to have those thoughts to prepare me WAY ahead of time for a death that would be my purgatory on Earth. But the thoughts don't end with Franko's death because as most Christians know, the Resurrection saved us, and death, as it is understood in the secular world, is no more. I believe with my deepest soul that I will see Frankie again. I HAVE to believe that because if there is nothingness after this life, how terribly sad would that be?

I beg God often to let me see him. The video I shared threw me for a loop! He was so real, so loving. He didn't want Jacob to have speech problems, so he helped him enunciate the word correctly. Frank was in speech therapy for five years, and HE pulled himself out! Yes, he realized a lot of kids graduated from speech therapy, and he was still there! I spoke with his therapist, and she admitted she just couldn't move him on because she loved him. She said he was special! He helped her with the kids! He was only in fifth grade.

Franko was no saint, and some people know more about that than his mom needs to know. But, with all my soul, I believe he is now! I ask him to pray for so many of us, especially his brothers. They miss him so much! I ask him to pray for his Dad with his huge decisions coming up. I ask him to pray for me because I miss him so much. It comforts me to talk to him, and I believe he hears his mother's cries!

If all of this is just someone's ideas from two-thousand-plus years ago, and they made up everything that I believe in, then they did a pretty darn good job...because...I'm convinced! It's all about the Lord! Peace! Franko, I love you! You know that, my Son!

7/21/18 early in the morning

Today... ah...today... happy...

Heavenly Birthday, Son, Frank Loret de Mola. This is NOT what I want to say. This is NOT what I want to say. THIS IS NOT WHAT I WANT TO SAY!

I can't imagine life without you, Son! I can't imagine growing older while you aren't here. I can't imagine it at all!

But when I'm in my quiet spot, whether it's in my car or in bed or wherever, I can talk, and I ask God to let me speak to you. What do I say? It's changed over the last ten months. I used to say, "COME BACK!" I used to beg God to take me and bring you back. I used to cry so hard and scream for you. But now...I tell you I love you. I ask you to pray for so many people: your brothers, your dad, your cousins and Grammy, extended family, his girlfriend and me. I ask for you to pray when your friends ask for prayers or good "vibes." I asked God permission to ask you for prayers. I know they are being heard.

So today is the first birthday without your whole self here, Franko. Dad and I miss you so much today. It is hard because thirty-four years ago, around this time, I started having contractions. We know that story, and about twelve hours later, you were born...six-thirty-ish in the evening. And you were the beautiful Son we thanked God for and loved beyond measure.

You are there. We are here. Give us strength to endure, Lord, as we make our way through this journey of grief and love.

Franko, Happy Birthday, my love.

We give this day to you, for you.

7/21/18

Today was a day... a first of many more to come. I loved seeing everyone, but I am wiped out. Weird how that happens!

AJ Johnson, thank you so much! You are beautiful inside and out! Thank you for helping me get through this day of Frank Loret de Mola's birth.

Stephanie, thank you for the incredible bruschetta! I need the recipe! Thank you!

Thank you to Chris, Frank's boss, for being a part. Thank you for the picture and all you do to keep Franko's memory alive!

Thank you to all my friends, my family, who brought WAY too much food! I love you!

Franko, Son. Jeff came, Frank's girlfriend and Niko too. Our friends Tatiana and Olga Amador came. Thank you!

Cheryl Richey, Carlota Agard, Ernesto D Agard, thank you so much! I love you guys!

Fr. Joshua Lickter came also, and your peaceful way was felt and always has been! Thank you!

Your friends meant so much to you, Son! They loved you almost as much as we do. Probably just as much, and that is the truth.

I love hearing stories about you, Franko! But sometimes it is also painful. Your loss has been taken hard by everyone who knew you!

Kevin Seppinni brought delicious gelato! He gave us your favorite chocolate type! He also gave us a vanilla one! Sooo delicious! So generous! Thank you, Kevin!

Emotions are running high...but you are worth any emotions I feel. I miss you and love you and still want you here. Since that isn't going to happen, I will celebrate you and your birth every year until I meet you in heaven. Not sure I could ever do another party, but you will always be with me! No one can take away the love of a mother and the child she gave birth to.

I love you, Franko. God bless you! Happy birthday! Sleep with the angels, in God's embrace!

Mom

7/22/18

God's blessings come in so many forms. Without hesitation, but maybe with a touch of nerves, three families united today because of love of one so giving of himself that his life has given life to people so deserving of this kind of love!

Today we met Polly Bleavins and Mac Daddy, her husband. They came from Santa Barbara to meet us and our closest friends. Polly received Franko's liver. Her life is AMAZING! She is beautiful and loving, and I am in awe of this beautiful couple! We laughed and shed a few tears, but the smiles and joy were in abundance! You are stuck with us for life, and we are now family, and I have another sister!

Today we met Gina Pak Dela Cruz, her husband Eugene Dela Cruz, their son Mason, and Gina's Aunt Robyn. Gina received one of Frank's kidney! They came from Pleasant Hill and spent the afternoon and evening with us, and it was the most amazing day! Gina is so beautiful, and her family is incredible! Love was bouncing off of all of us and even the walls! I didn't want to let go of either of the girls! I thank God this day happened!

Carlota Agard, Ernesto D Agard, Nancy Tran, Nick Tran, JC Tran, Jada Tran, and Tony NaRanong shared this day with my mom (Laura Loebe) and Enrique Loret de Mola and me. How can I ever say enough about how much I appreciate the love and laughter we shared? We WILL do this again!

I am wired for sound and need to go to bed!

Thank You, God, for this incredible day! Thank you, our beautiful Son, for the love you continue to give!

Wow!

Polly, liver Recipient; me; Gina, kidney recipient; Henry, Frank's dad

7/24/18

I am just in awe of God's plans! Seriously, none of us could have ever put this weekend together if we had tried to do this all by ourselves!

Tears began our Saturday morning, and by the end of that day, smiles and laughter permeated the walls of our home. Frank's birthday was perfect!

Yesterday was a day I will never forget! Ever! The tears turned to great joy within minutes of meeting our new extended family! WOW! Beautiful! I know I use the word beautiful a lot, but truly...it was a beautiful day!

If you aren't a donor, don't be afraid. The heartache and pain of losing such an incredible life turns to pure love when you realize the gift your loved one gave was nothing but love for another to begin again! It is incredible!

I am so proud to be the mother of Frank Loret de Mola! I am so thankful!

God be with us all as we go through the next years ahead. One step at a time!

7/24/18

I slept until 8:00 A.M.! I don't do that often.

I came downstairs, and Enrique Loret de Mola had been reading some journals AJ Johnson had given to David Loret de Mola to see. Frank wrote in them from time to time, and tears flowed.

My tears were painful, yet joy-filled. My tears were longing for our son, but in two seconds I was laughing at his humor. My tears were for what won't happen and for the incredible man he still is in my heart. My tears are breathless, yet breathing in and savoring ANYTHING Frank Loret de Mola! Thank you, AJ, for this treasure...this incredible reminder of our love. Wow!

Peace, Son! Your depth in this life was beyond your age number! You bring me to my knees in awe of the gift you gave...yourself...wide open for all to see! Rest and continue creating love! I know you are!

Mom

7/27/18

Our son, David Loret de Mola, posted poetry about love and said, "I love you." I have been thinking about how I say I love you a lot. I mean it every time I say it.

I have friends I love and, of course, family I love. When I tell someone I love them, it means more than a friendship. It means you are a part of my heart, a part of my family. Your place in my life has meaning, and you are going to have a spot that is deeper and special.

Every person I love has a unique and different relationship with me. I am so thankful for that because I might be more serious with some of you and more to playful with others. I might pray with some of you and have a glass of wine with others. This is the light and beauty of such incredible and wonderful friendships!

So, to all of my family and family of friends...I love you!

Thanks, David, for my food for thought today!

More Frank Notes 7/28/18

For some reason, today was a hard day! I felt like crying and did a little. I know why my heart felt sad today, but there was an ache I just couldn't figure out.

Mom and I got out of the house, thinking I was having a bit of stir-crazy feelings. We figured we'd go shopping and maybe I would get rid of my "cabin fever." We had just walked into Ross and Mom got a phone call that one of her best friends has seventy-two hours to live. I KNOW I was sensing something but didn't know until the call as to why I was feeling this sadness all morning.

Frank Loret de Mola used to tell me I had a sixth sense. I call it God preparing me.

You know, I did feel better. I felt relieved and peace because I know where my mom's friend is going. She will meet her oldest son. She will meet our son. She will meet God! And so many others! I believe that! I have to because I want the same someday!

7/28/18

Since the loss of Frank Loret de Mola, people, especially at church, know how I have said yes to helping only to back out even at the last minute. Am I just lazy? I don't think so. Am I just a pain in the butt? Probably, but I just can't get motivated. Am I going through major grief? I guess so, but this is NOTHING I have ever gone through before, so the feelings I have are so foreign!

When my friend Gayle Delos Reyes was dying in 1984 and I helped take care of her, I was so happy to spend time with her! After her death, I was so depressed, but I didn't realize it. About a month after she was gone, Henry asked me to see our PA Julie because he could see I needed some help. Julie said to me, and I will never forget, "Jackie! What do you expect? Your husband has been in Russia working a lot, you have 4 children, you put things aside to take care of your friend, and now she's gone! Of course, you are depressed!" She gave me an antidepressant, and in three months I was able to get off of it and I did great!

And now...and now...this is so different and foreign, as if there is an object in my eye I can't remove. Must be my tears! Nope...it's my Son.

I know I am a different person today. Anyone who has lost a child understands this...but I am getting through it BECAUSE of God's Grace!

Am I getting help, you might ask? Yes. But truly, this is a journey I understand to be full of pain but beauty. This path is blessed but trying. I am going through something now that I almost welcome because when it gets lots better, and it will, I will understand the ride and appreciate this life more!

7/30/18

Just when I think I'm ready for bed...tears come. The tears come out of nowhere but heartache, from missing my Son, Frank Loret de Mola. Missing his intelligence and ways of understanding this old Mom. Kind of mad...because it feels like forever ago, but it's only been a little more than ten months. Feels like forever until I will meet him, if I am worthy to be with him! I'm trying my best, but I have a lot of work to do! I will work harder! I will keep

God foremost in my mind so I never forget Who this life is all about. Dear Creator, please don't do this to me ever again! I don't think I could lose another child and remain human! Sometimes I feel like I don't feel!

I know I'm doing pretty good most of the time, but it's those unexpected emotions that catch me off guard and expose my soul. I am laid open and exposed to the rawest of emotions. Out of control. But I regain myself...putting the pieces left of me together again and kissing Frank's picture on my phone as if he can feel it! I would like to believe he can. I'm allowed to think this way...

7/31/18

I never ever used to question God. But I have often in the past ten months... Oh not constantly, but just wanting to understand how someone with so much going on in his life could be gone so quickly. Nope, it's not fair at all, but I accept it and will grow from this.

7/31/18

As Enrique Loret de Mola was leaving for work, he said, "Una ves mas...." his last day to work at the facility he has driven to for the past MULTIPLE years...He will set up an "office" in our bedroom for the next month, and then this part of his life will be done. He would like to work still, but that might not happen, at least with the company he's been with for almost forty years! I said he needs a retirement party...but that's not something he wants.

He began in 1979 with EDS, Electronic Data Systems. It has been sold to numerous companies, such as GM, HP, and now DXC...I am his wife, and I can say...it's not like the company he began with...

Henry's heyday was when we lived in Michigan! His job was huge, and there was prestige to it. That was when Ross Perot sold to GM, then bought it back when he saw it wasn't going in the direction he thought it would, AND GM didn't see things like Mr. Perot either...

There were lots of changes through the years, but one thing remained... Henry's dedication to his job and his family! I have been blessed to be his wife and trust God's will in all our multiple moves...state to state...sometimes one town to the next!

Henry has seen so much in his life, from Cuba to the US. as a refugee at the age of ten (his sister Sandra Sluss was fourteen)...sent to get away from an oppressive regime...His mom was brilliant and knew way more than many who stayed.

Henry joined the army and became a citizen of this incredible country! He married me, and four sons were his blessing. Even the pain of the loss of Frank Loret de Mola has taken its toll, but Henry continued to go to work, as it seemed to help him keep his mind busy to get beyond...

This man is not your norm! He loves his sons and me beyond words, and his grandchildren are the smiles he finds. How did all of this happen? God's grace and prayerful hope in God providing for this family.

Thank you, Babe, for all you have done and do for all of us! We would be nothing without you. God gave you to me, and we give it all back to God!

It will be weird for a while, having us both home all the time...but we will adjust, as you said!

Here's to you, Enrique Loret de Mola!

I love you!

8/1/18

Okay...so I had ROUGH day, but I also have to say, the cloud lifted and I am way better! I guess this journey of grief is unpredictable and profound! I love it because of the parts of my soul I am finding. But I HATE it because of the WHY I have to go through this!

FRANKtitude forever!

Love of family forever!

Peace be with you forever!

8/1/18

This was the second thing I saw today! Believe it or not... I needed this! Facebook said it looks like Frank and I spent a lot of time together! Funny, some of my last thoughts before I fell asleep last night were, I didn't spend enough time with you, Franko! Then this! My heart feels good! Thanks, Facebook, for making me smile!

8/1/18

Here are pictures of Franko making coffee, and I wrote:

"Allison, a friend of Franko's, posted pictures of him today...Breathless! Sharing! Oh how I miss you!"

8/3/18

Someone shared a post of a video with three girls in a car and the driver is texting...I really had a hard time with it...I wrote: "Too hard to watch... jaws of life were needed for Franko. I wasn't there, but I can imagine. I wish I was there to say goodbye...to hold him...he might have still been able to hear me crying for him...screaming for him... this one is all too real for me! Can't share it...

8/9/18

I haven't written about Franko much lately...I have him tucked away deep inside my heart and soul. I am beginning to feel joy again. I mean, real joy and happiness. I still get heart palpitations when I try to fall asleep, and I think of his beautiful face, and I pray. I ask God to help me. I ask Mary to help me, and I ask Franko to pray for me. I think he is because I feel lighter, and peaceful, and ready to find more of this each day! I love you Frank Loret de Mola forever and ever! You are the sunlight at 5:30 A.M. and the moon at 9:00 P.M. You are in my thoughts always, and I believe you are praying for your old mom and dad, brothers, and so many others! Life has changed so significantly since you left this planet, but I am adjusting because I KNOW you can hear me from afar, and if you can't, please let me know so I can speak louder!

I love you!
Mom

8/15/18

At the foot of Your cross, I place my breathlessness...
At the foot of Your cross, I give my longing...
At the foot of Your cross, I grieve with You...
At the foot of Your cross, I understand more why...
At the foot of Your cross, I rest in You, oh Lord...

8/16/18

Sometimes, when I watch the news or see a show or someone posts something on Facebook about a car accident, I do fine. But last night I realized I can cry and cry some more over your loss, Frank Loret de Mola. Henry rubbed my back and shoulders. I couldn't do this without my husband, Enrique Loret de Mola! I love you!

Just can't believe how things affect me now. I want to scream at reckless drivers swerving in and out of cars. I want to scream when I see people flip each other off because of a true mistake made while driving. I even saw two men getting out of their cars yelling about something that ALMOST happened. I began having heart palpitations because I was next to them!

I want to create a sign I can hold up when I see people driving crazy that reads, "MY SON WAS KILLED BECAUSE SOMEONE DROVE LIKE YOU!" But I won't. I know that is not going to help selfish drivers.

I wonder how Michael Sanchez is doing...I wonder how the people in front of Franko's car are doing. I wonder how everyone in Frank's life are doing. As for me, I'm still on the mend. Obviously!

Tears came last night, and I fell asleep crying and thanking God for life and love!

At times, I still feel...*wake me when it's over!*

But I am fine and will move forward because Frank would NEVER EVER want me worrying about him! I don't. I KNOW where he is! Heavenly...

8/21/18

I really didn't want to walk again, but I pushed myself. Once I got outside, I loved it! I could have worn a light jacket. So beautiful! I listened to and prayed a beautiful Rosary, as I do when I walk. Tears flowed for just a bit, but then peace filled my heart. I know our Savior is truly holding me in this journey of love, forgiveness, and hope.

Frank Loret de Mola, Son, you were not killed in vain. You brought life to more than the four people blessed with health. You brought love to so many who still can't believe you are out of this world and will continue to love with greater fervor because of your death. What more do we need to realize how fast life goes? What more do we need to find a gentle God Who truly is there for the broken-hearted? I cannot go through this alone in my thoughts of aching and longing for you. I believe the Blessed Mother desires all of her children to ask her for prayers!

After you died, Franko, I asked Mary to take care of you and to hold you. I find comfort, great comfort, in my belief that she is doing just that!

Will I ever stop missing you? I doubt it, but the ache is less as my faith kicks in and allows me to truly grow from all of this. I thank God for you, Son, and I forever will!

Amen! Alleluia!

8/28/18

Tonight Henry and I ate at Toby Keith's and really enjoyed our dinner. We had a great talk, and Henry said something that made me feel so sad for him…He said he was looking forward to spending retirement time with all the boys…but we are missing one. I'm not sad like…depressed…just sad that he really was looking forward to having a cup of coffee with Frank Loret de Mola. We also talked about showing up in Seattle to bug Alex Loret de Mola and Allie Criado! Don't worry, we'd call ahead! We know we will see Nick Loret de Mola and David Loret de Mola unless we move back to Tucson. The way California is going, we may have no choice but to get away from all the taxes!

We really did have a nice dinner just spending "downtime" together!

Leaving to get back to Sacramento in the morning…

Fun and expensive trip. It's called lost wages for a darn good reason! Never again!

8/29/18

Just got home...

I wrote this on the plane...

It always surprises me when tears begin. I'm sitting on the plane, looking at Franko's pictures, and still not quite believing he isn't going to come to visit. He isn't going to call and say, "Hey Ma!" He isn't going to give me one of his famous hugs. He isn't. He isn't. He isn't. WHY??? WHY???? Oh God WHY!!! I miss him something awful right now, and it came on so suddenly. Like my heart broke open, and the tears flooded my face.

I suppose this is how things are going to be now. I feel alone even though Henry is right beside me. I feel the pain of your death, Franko, as if it happened today. I don't like feeling this way, but it's real and raw, and my wounds are huge. I just need to see you and hug you and tell you how life isn't the same since you left us. I'm sure each person who knew and loved you sees you in a different way. But I, Your Mother, I...I...feel like I can't go on without you anymore. I can't. But I will. Because I love you, and you would want me to move on—not necessarily forward—just on. I think I can most days. But not right now. I'm tired of being strong. I'm tired of seeming to be fine when in my gut, my inmost being, I'm still screaming for you! COME HOME! Come back! But you can't, and I have to really get that through my head. You aren't coming back. But I will meet you there, if God will have me in all my sinfulness. Please be there when it's my turn, okay?

I love you, Franko!

8/30/18

Is it weird to feel closer to Franko when I'm on a plane? I do...Now I'm grounded again...missing him something fierce. Is it because it's almost been a year? Is it because I have so much I want to say? Is it because there's a huge void that time might be able to heal, but I doubt it!

Another day...

Please God, help my sadness and wake me when it's over! The fog came back, and I don't quite know the trigger. But God will see me through!

I will be back in the sky on a plane soon…Pray for me, please. I know my family and friends do! Thank you! I love you all!

I miss you, Frank Loret de Mola. With every ounce of my being, I miss you!

9/1/18

I think of you so much. This THING we are going through, to put it mildly, SUCKS! I melt down, get back up, only to melt down again! My heart is partly in heaven and partly on earth. My thoughts go from joy of memories to tears of longing. How could we be going through this? How could a young man with so much to live for be stripped away at such a young age? I ask God that all the time…all the time!

Nancy, I speak to Frankie all the time! I ask him to pray for me. I know he does. He isn't a saint, but, like Tony, they are VERY close! We are truly blessed that our sons showed the world their love and greatness! And how loved they are and were!

Nancy, the class of '73 will have a get together on October 20th. Info below. I'm thinking I will drive there in early October and stay for a while. Think about coming, okay?

I love you so much my sister friend.

Jack

9/3/18

I've been awake since a bit after 3 A.M. Same thoughts, Franko…always…

So, I got up, came downstairs, and opened my email to find JUST what I needed! I'll post it below. Maybe we all need this.

We all go through darkness, whether it is a lost kitten, an aging parent, a job layoff, sickness, or the death of a child, and so many other reasons we find ourselves in darkness, but it happens. This, the thing we have been going through, possibly too publicly, hit me again at three-ish. The loss of my son will always be with me. I know that. But I can choose to live in darkness until I die or find even a small light glowing. Even in a dark room, one flame of a match can illuminate the space. Can I find that one small flicker left in me? YES! Not only will I find the flicker, I will see the glow and continue to spread it and BE it!

I have to!

I have Enrique Loret de Mola and Nick Loret de Mola and Alex Loret de Mola and David Loret de Mola; my beautiful grandkids, my mom, and all my family and friends to live with and for. And I have this God person helping me to live!

So...please read what I found FIRST thing this morning and find that light in your darkness too!

Love to all!

Never forget in the light what you learn in the darkness.

Father, help those who are hurting today so they may see and know Your loving presence in their darkest hours.

9/10/18

I posted this last year...if only I would have known then, to prepare my heart for what was to come. It seemed the miracle I prayed for beginning September 20th was not a visible miracle, but miracles in other forms. Frank Loret de Mola, you are the blessing to so many. I reach out to you in prayer. I speak to you in the silence of any space I'm in. I hold you in my heart and thank God for your life.

9/10/18

Megan Bliss, me too...crying now and praying. I miss you, Frank Loret de Mola, and I have a feeling you miss us too. I just can't believe a year is almost over. I thought it was a long dream or nightmare, but I think I'm awake and warm tears fall easily still. I think they always will.

Psalm 34:18 says, "The Lord is close to the brokenhearted and saves those who are crushed in spirit."

Jesus, help me! I beg You, God, ease my sadness because the moments before I sleep are the hardest in each day. I know You alone, Lord, can fill my empty heart. Fill it with love for my sons, husband, family, and friends, and let me be thankful for beautiful memories, and some painful ones too. All of my life's journey has kept me growing towards You, Lord—even the most awful times. I praise You God! Amen!

Goodnight!

9/10/18 more

This is too real still.

Losing Frank made death more real. The events of 9/11 made horrible people more real than ever before. Let's never forget, but let's really learn from our past.

Where are we headed? What does life have in store? Do we care? Are we hopeful? Do we live to serve others? Are we trying to help our families be happy? Do we believe there is something to guide us? So much uncertainty. Lead us, Lord. I am willing to follow, God. Just give me answers to help our world and give those same answers to all!

9/12/18

As my family and I get closer to the year anniversary of Frank Loret de Mola's death, a song brings me both comfort and sadness. Sadness because the reality is still unbelievable. Comfort because I sing from the depth of my heart knowing that what I truly believe will bring me back to you, Son! I love you, Franko!

9/16/18

Text message to Alex:

> "I miss you Son! Can you believe it's almost a year since Frank's accident? My heart is aching but I'm okay. Still in Michigan visiting Lori and all. God has truly gotten us all through this year! I have gone to the depths of sadness and suffering unlike anything I ever want to do again. But this life is just temporary and sometimes we have to see our lives changed in a second. Nothing is the same, yet everything still remains in this life. I love you, your brothers, and Dad now more than ever! Can't wait for the wedding and the joy that will fill the air! I love you! Kiss Allie! I love her so much!

9/17/18

We all have changes in our lives. Sometimes those changes are filled with joy and awe. But sometimes those changes bring unending tears and sadness. This has been a year for all!

Never in my life would I have ever thought that Enrique Loret de Mola and I would grow old without our Son, Frank Loret de Mola! NEVER! Never would I have thought our sons would be without their brother! NEVER!

But it happened. It is real. And the year that I felt I was dying from a broken heart will happen soon. It's been 364 days without you, Franko. This "new normal" thing sucks, to be honest. However, our sons and grandkids, family and friends bring love and hope.

Can't believe we are almost at the twentieth to the twenty-second of September. It is real. I just want it to still be just a bad dream.

9/19/18
MORNING OFFERING

September 19, 2018

"The closer one approaches to God, the simpler one becomes."

— St. Teresa of Avila

Find love in the simple. That is how I see this quote from St. Teresa of Avila. Downsize. Renew thoughts. Live FRANKtitude daily!

9/20/18...it's been a year...

A year of fog that lifts and sets in after the turbulence of a life being taken.

A year of family and friends in complete disbelief that such a thing could really happen.

If he was okay, he would have called and said, "Don't worry Mom and Dad. I'm okay!" Never got that call. Sometimes I still wait for it.

My tears come, not as strong as a day ago, and not as overwhelming as September 20, 2017. And I doubt they will ever stop.

For me, the one who gave birth to four incredible sons, losing a child is losing a piece of my entire being. It's not "LIKE" losing a piece of my entire being. It IS losing a piece of my entire being.

I don't write these things for comments. I don't write these words for admonishment or praise. I don't write my thoughts for people to love me more or remove me from their lists. I write my thoughts in order to keep Frank Loret de Mola, Frank Anthony Loret de Mola, alive! If I speak his name, somehow, he remains. If I share all of this, he becomes alive to me.

My heart gets pasted all over this site so that Frank's life continues. I can't let him go. I just can't. And I know many moms who understand this all too well.

I love you, Son, and each day I will do my best to keep you alive. FRANKtitude, forever...

9/21/18

MORNING OFFERING
September 21, 2018
"For me, prayer is a surge of the heart; it is a simple look turned toward heaven, it is a cry of recognition and of love, embracing both trial and joy."
— St. Therese of Lisieux

9/21/18

And then there's this...Read Frank Loret de Mola's response to my comment! Lord, is this how it's going to be now that we are so close to the year since Frank left? My heart is beating at a rapid pace. Oh, how I love you! Oh, how I miss you!

9/22/18

This is painful to read, especially for me...I wrote it...I continue to grow from this point, only falling back a few steps. Today I am still in disbelief that this is our reality, but I am accepting the truth a bit better.

"Never regret anything about family and friends. Trust that God will get you through any issues and battles we have with people we love. Fight and resolve. Get angry at stupid things, but realize how silly those things are to our relationships. Laugh, even if it seems ridiculous, because laughter truly does find a place for healing. And love...LOVE like tomorrow is your last day. I don't necessarily mean sexual, although that is perfect too. I mean love with a heart of God. See no imperfections. See no color or race. See no differences at all. Just love."

I so wish September 22, 2017 had never happened...but it did. What have I learned? Ask yourself that too...and come to a realization that Frank's life truly mattered. His absence does too. A man such as our Son continues to leave his legacy. What a gift he is still.

I smile at memories I have recently had and cry because...well...you know.

A year is done. A year of incredible highs and extreme lows. Through it all, my faith is stronger because I believe, with all my heart and soul, that Frank will be there to show me heaven when my turn comes!

I love all of my sons, now more than life! I love you, Enrique Loret de Mola, deeply and forever!

Jesus, I place my trust in eternity! I place my hope in You, Lord!

I love you, Frank Loret de Mola!

Amen! And Alleluia!

Posted with the above post, what I wrote a year ago on this date:

"Oh God I want him back NOW!!!! GOD! CAN YOU HEAR ME? Believers and non-believers alike can unite in this...WE LOVE THIS HUMAN BEING! THIS INCREDIBLE MAN MY SON Frank Loret de Mola! Why is he going? I know we were not meant to live in this form on Earth forever...but I know and I believe that we continue to be a part of each other's lives after we aren't on this planet any longer. BUT...WHY AT 33 YEARS OF AGE DOES HE HAVE TO GO? Does someone know why? The answer isn't easy. The answer isn't something anyone can easily grasp. The answer is far too deep to WANT to believe it. But if I didn't believe in a life Eternal...what is left? I will be so bold to say...I know I will see Frank, our son, in my dreams. I know I will see Frank, our son, when I am at a grocery store or walking down the street and someone is walking like him or looks like him or has his heart, kidneys, or his skin. And do you know what I will see? Love...joy...smiles from our son. My pain is so real. I cannot sleep. My heart is laid open. I cannot imagine life without you, Franko. My ears hear your laughter when you and your brothers are enjoying your time together...loudly! My soul begs God to not take you...Take me instead!

SO...NO ANSWERS TO WHY? This beautiful man we call Son, Brother, Lover, Friend, has left a beautiful legacy of love, peace, harmony, truth, encouragement, and joy like we have never known...I call all of that God...known to me through the sons I gave birth to. I call Franko a Jesus living and walking, a belief and love of humanity. I call Franko a Holy Spirit person who blessed his family and friends with memories to continue his legacy of love in action.

I call him life.

Amen!

9/22/18

Julianne Averbuck, I don't remember seeing this post from last year...Thank you, Cousin. It was my first memory in my Facebook, and I feel the peace! Ocean water is healing for me! Thank you! I love you! Julie Anne asked for prayers for the Loebe and Loret de Mola family and posted a pic of the ocean on 9/22/17....

9/22/18

The doorbell rang just now. Flowers and chocolates received. The note...my heart is racing...Michael Sanchez, I believe...the young man who hit Frank's car, and I am breathless! I am in awe and thanking God for this...mixed feelings for sure...but forgiveness is real and permanent. Wow! Totally unexpected! He was blessed by the decision for leniency, and we are blessed to have had a part in that decision. Jesus, I trust in You and your providence in our lives! Continue praying for Michael and all who can't forgive yet. It is okay to forgive and mean it! I have! Wow!

10/3/18

As I lay here in this bed in Tucson, Arizona, awake since before 2:00 A.M...I am reading so many quotes from so many people. Megan Bliss, you posted one that brought back a song to my heart, a song my friend Michael John Poirier wrote so many years ago. I know his reasons for writing this song, but my reasons for never forgetting it have changed through the years. This song takes on new meaning for me and gives me goosebumps.

I used to sing this song for many funerals years ago. I sing it this early morning as a mantra for letting my pain and hurt go...Fly to the heavens all you pain and hurt...Release me from the sadness that can still overwhelm me in moments so unexpected. This song fills me and brings the Resurrection closer to me than ever before.

Michael John Poirier wrote the lyrics and music to "Break the Chains":

> Oh Lord, my God, I trust in Thee
> To be my true and lasting peace.
> Oh Lord, my God, I trust in Thee
> To be my true and lasting peace.
> Oh Lord, my God, I long for Thee
> Come break the chains, still binding me.

Oh Lord, my God, I long for Thee
Come break the chains, still binding me.

Please just take a few minutes, in a quiet place, and meditate on Michael's music...You might find peace...I have...Break the Chains...

Father Joshua Lickter, Enrique Loret de Mola, and I had lunch, and we spoke about the Resurrection. Fr. Josh, thank you for the beautiful "lesson" at the table...to understand Jesus is to know the Resurrection. Yes...and there is hope, for we who believe, that we will see our loved ones again!

10/11/18

Just a mom missing her son!

2/22/19

A huge part of my healing was hearing from Henry that he had met and hugged the young man who caused the car accident that killed our son. I wasn't present for the second arraignment because I went to Tucson to heal.

We wanted leniency, and Michael was given three years of probation and a misdemeanor. We went to several hearings prior to the final resolution.

I thank God because the forgiveness freed me from thinking about the way our son was killed. Someone told me, "Don't keep replaying the accident in your head. You weren't there. Remember, he died once. Not over and over again."

That was HUGE advice! I stopped putting myself at the scene. I stopped seeing him helpless in his new car. It gave me better perspective!

Forgive those who have hurt you.

Don't replay the pain! It happened, and as long as you can forgive, try hard to forgive.

Ask God for the grace to forgive.

God gave me my healing heart!

Thanks be to God!

2/26/19

Yes! We know pain and love God anyway! He didn't bring Frank back, but He did bring me back from the greatest despair I have ever known. And do you know what? It could happen again and again and again. He is a real God to me. He cried with me. As did His Mother Mary.

3/27/19

They say time heals the brokenhearted. Who are they? Yes, I don't cry as hard. I don't stay in bed all day. I don't get in a fetal position anymore.

But I do miss our son each and every day and all day. I doubt that will ever change.

I have friends who have lost a child many years ago. They still cry. I have family and friends who have miscarried a baby or more than one, and they cry. Still. I get it!

I have written this book because I felt a huge need to do something concrete to remember Franko. He would have written something about this too...I believe that! Only he might have found some kind of weird humor in the journey.

If my journey has helped you, please message me on Facebook. I am Jackie Loebe Loret de Mola. If you have stories about Frank, please tell me! If you hate the book, it's okay. It isn't for the faint of heart. I almost died of a broken heart. I really understand how that is possible. I am sure I aged in front of my family. And that is okay too.

God bless all who are struggling with loss. It isn't easy. It isn't supposed to be. Just know that you are not alone. Reach out and ask for help. Reach out and let God hold you through the process. Take time for yourself, and allow all the time in the world.

With love from a mother who is continuing this journey,

Jackie

CPSIA information can be obtained
at www.ICGtesting.com
Printed in the USA
LVHW080146210720
661172LV00015B/214